TRACK AND FIELD EVENTS

Fundamentals

THE MERRILL SPORTS SERIES

under the editorship of
Lewis A. Hess
The Ohio State University

TRACK AND FIELD EVENTS

Fundamentals

Richard Bowers
Bowling Green State University

CHARLES E. MERRILL PUBLISHING COMPANY
A Bell & Howell Company
Columbus, Ohio 43216

Published by
Charles E. Merrill Publishing Company
A Bell & Howell Company
Columbus, Ohio 43216

Library of Congress Catalog Card Number: 73-83432

International Standard Book Number: 0-675-08893-3

2 3 4 5 6 7 8 9 10—77 76

Illustrations by Carlos Cobbs

Printed in the United States of America

Foreword

THE MERRILL SPORTS SERIES has been developed with two primary objectives in mind. First, to improve the teaching and learning of sports and secondly, to assist those who wish to develop or improve their knowledges, understandings, and competence in a variety of sports. These publications are in keeping with the modern educational trend, which places more responsibility on the individual for his learning, growth, and development. The development of a satisfactory proficiency in the area of sports involves a series of complex learning experiences. To use the best available learning processes it is essential that as many avenues of learning as possible be brought into play. This involves reading, listening, visualizing, observing, and actual participation. These texts take this into consideration so that the student has an opportunity to learn in depth and profit from learning cues developed by highly competent teachers.

This series will provide challenge and enjoyment in a variety of sports activities. Competence in a sport will be improved in terms of knowledges, appreciations, and performance. Likewise, the more experienced student will find the publications a source of information in developing a higher level of proficiency. In our society one cannot claim to be "educated" unless he possesses a level of knowledge and performance in a number of sports which can play an important role in the use of his leisure time and the maintenance of his general well-being.

An effort has been made through the presentation of well illustrated, explained, and logically arranged analysis of skills and highly effective methods of instruction to assist in the understanding of the nature of the activity, the skills of the activity, and the ability to evaluate personal progress or development with relation to the activity. Each volume is meant to be an addition to one's personal library as a lasting source of information. The material covered is of

v

such depth that participation will be enhanced along with an appreciation of a variety of sports' activities so important in our present leisure-oriented society.

The authors are highly educated and thoroughly experienced teachers and performers. They have made an effort to present teaching and learning techniques specific to each sport which have been proven optimum methods of acquiring skills, knowledges, and understandings involved in participation of the particular activity. The use of the series, coupled with professional instruction, will result in achieving a more self-satisfying educational experience which should not only speed up the learning process, but should improve one's enjoyment of leisure time.

Lewis A. Hess
Editor

Preface

Track and Field Events was written primarily for use in physical education classes. However, the serious track and field athlete can find useful ideas and concepts for his use in it as well. Although in most instances one method of learning an event is presented, this, of course, does not preclude the use of any other method. I have simply tried to use the descriptions and explanations that have worked best for me as both an assistant coach at the university level for nine years and as a practicing physical educator.

One of the unique features of this volume is the performance table found in the Appendix. It is unique in that performance standards are based on the results of the efforts of eighteen and nineteen-year-old, nonvarsity-level, male track and field participants. Raw data were collected over a period of five years from physical education classes. The events included are those that I have found to be *most practical* in a physical education setting. The scale score (0-100) is based upon the *The Hull Scale* ($\pm$ 3.5 standard deviations). Except in the possible exceptions of the 880-meter or one-mile runs, it would be the very rare individual who could score 100 points on the scale score because, in most cases the athlete would have to be performing at world-record levels to achieve such a feat.

My involvement in track and field, both as an athlete and as a coach, has been a most rewarding one for me. It is my hope that through this book, I can, in some small way, share the good experiences and sense of deep satisfaction that I have known to others.

Richard Bowers

To My Wife Carolyn
and
To Our Two Children
Katie Kim and David Scott

Contents

The Running Events And Hurdling

1

Sprinting

Sprinting, or running for speed, is one of man's most natural activities; it has been a part of his existence for thousands of years. In the days of the cave man, sprinting was a necessity of life both for escaping enemies and for pursuing animals for food. Over the centuries, this activity gradually has changed from a necessary part of survival to a game of sport. The first significant evidence of sprinting as sport appeared in ancient Greece. In the early Greek games, the only race was the *stade*, or a sprint the length of the stadium, which varied in distance from 200 to 240 yards. Later, the *diaulos*, or two-length race, was added.

Today, sprint races include distances of anywhere from fifty to 440 yards. The standard distances for indoor competition are sixty and 300 yards; other distances, such as fifty and seventy yards, also may be run depending upon the space available. When races are held outdoors, sprint distances include 100, 220, and 440 yards. The 440-yard dash becomes a sprint race only on the very high levels of competition.

Elements of Sprinting

Broken down into its components, sprinting consists of three phases: the start, the sprint, and the finish.

Getting Started

Starting blocks are used almost universally today, yet as recently as the days of Jesse Owens (mid 1930s), the athletes dug holes in the track at the "scratch" line and braced their feet in these holes. Except for the acceptance of starting blocks in the late 1930s, starting techniques have not changed a great deal in the past fifty years.

There are essentially three types of starts: *the elongated start,* where the back foot is at least eighteen inches from the front foot in the starting blocks; *the bunch start,* in which the two feet are very close together (approximately ten to twelve inches apart) and close to the starting line; and *the medium start,* in which the back foot is twelve to eighteen inches from the front foot in the starting block. The medium start generally is accepted as being the best to learn initially; it can be modified slightly later to meet the needs of the individual athlete. It has been determined experimentally that the medium start allows the athlete to develop the greatest power when starting. This last concept is very significant because in starting a sprint race, the athlete is trying to overcome resting inertia; that is, he is trying to *accelerate* to his top *speed* in as short a time as possible.

To Your Marks. This order is the first of several well-defined instructions for starting a race. Each command is followed by a specific maneuver of the athlete.

Runners, Stand at Your Marks. At this time, the athlete will have removed his warm-up suit and is standing behind his blocks.

Take Your Marks. How the athlete approaches this phase of the start is very important. He should step forward, then place his hands on the track in front of the starting line. At this point, many sprinters like to extend each leg and shake it slightly before settling down into the blocks. After the feet are placed on the blocks,[1] the hands are placed as close to the starting line as possible with the fingers bridged. The effect of the bridge is to place the shoulders as high as possible. The sprinter then relaxes his head and presses forward in the blocks so that his shoulders are just over the starting line (see Figure 1.1).

At this instant, an observer would see the sprinter with the knee of his *back* leg resting on the ground, his fingers bridged and barely touching the ground at a point just wider than shoulder width, and his body pressed forward with his shoulders slightly over the starting line. The head is relaxed and bent downward slightly. The sprinter is now ready for the "set" command.

Set. At this command, the sprinter raises his hips to just above shoulder level, thereby putting most of his weight on his straight arms

---

[1] The toes of the shoes must touch the ground.

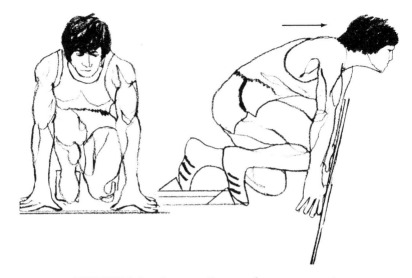

FIGURE 1.1.   *Starting Position from Two Angles*

and the forward leg. If his arms were lifted from the track at this time, he would fall forward on his face. During this very important stage, an observer could make the following observations: the shoulders of the sprinter extend over the starting line by one to two inches; arms are straight but not locked in a hyperextended position; the knee of the front leg is bent at about 90 degrees while the back leg is bent at an angle between 115 degrees and 120 degrees; the hips are positioned so that they are slightly higher than shoulder level; finally, the head is in such a position that the eyes are focused about three to five *feet* down the track.

Go.   Usually, the starter has a starting pistol and the race begins with the report of that pistol. At the start, the athlete's entire concentration is focused on the first move he will make. His immediate re-action is to lift both arms from the track and simultaneously begin to drive straight forward with both legs. The back leg comes off the block first and next touches the ground about twenty-four inches in front of the starting line, while the other leg is being completely extended from the hips to the tips of the runner's toes. By this time, the rhythmic, pistonlike action of the arms is being coordinated with the driving, lifting knees. The arms are driven very vigorously in an uppercut motion with each step. The body gradually assumes an upright position as the stride lengthens until full stride is reached about twenty-five to thirty-five yards from the starting line.

Form and Finish

During the middle part of the race, the athlete is running in a straight line in a nearly erect posture. The knees are being lifted and the arms are swinging diagonally in an upward, across-the-body motion; *however*, the arms are not allowed to cross the midline. As the knee lifts, it is brought straight down to the track, and as the foot comes in contact with the ground, the leg drives the sprinter forward by extending fully.

FIGURE 1.2.   *Running Style*

Many sprinters defeat themselves in a race because of muscular tension. Tension in a sprinter can be seen by watching the tight, jerky swing of arms or tensed muscles in shoulders and neck. A "tight" runner will have what appears to be a very pained, drawn expression on his face, with the neck veins appearing to "pop out." The experienced, confident sprinter shows almost no expression on his face; his jaw and shoulders appear to be relaxed.

In order to win a race, the athlete's torso must be the first to cross the finish line. Because of this fact, many sprinters lean forward on the last two strides. Nonetheless, the essential thing is for the sprinter to maintain good running form for as long as possible so that his speed is not impaired during the race. It is generally agreed that a forward lean at the last moment is beneficial to a sprinter; however, many sprinters lose a close race when they lean too early and thus reduce their forward drive.

The Long Sprints: 220, 300, 440

Contrary to popular feelings, the long sprints of from 220 yards up to 440 yards require stamina as well as natural sprinting speed. This requirement is more obvious at 440 yards than it is at 220 yards.

The 220 and 300

As with the 100-yard dash, it is important to concentrate on starting, good form during the race, and a strong finish in the 220-yard sprint. For instructions on starting, the reader is referred to pp. 3 and 4.

During the middle part of the race, the athlete in the 220 and 300 should learn to run in a more relaxed manner than he would during the 100, but, at the same time, he should maintain speed. This relaxed running is referred to as the "float" and may last for as short a distance as twenty yards or as long as fifty yards depending on the circumstances. In a preliminary heat, where the runner knows he also will be running one or two later races, the float can be of longer duration, but in the finals, the floating period may be very short because all contestants will be of a high calibre and intent upon winning.

The 440-Yard Dash

Up until a few years ago, the 440 was referred to as the 440-yard "run." However, athletes have become so well trained that the 440 has been removed from the realm of "running" and placed in the category of "sprinting." Analyzing the current world record of 44.5 seconds, we see that the average time for each 100 yards is just slightly over 10 seconds! This time would be a very respectable one for the 100-yard dash.

Floating becomes very important in the 440. During the middle 100 yards or so, "relaxing" at top speed is essential. The 440 runner who lacks the ability to relax during the race invariably will develop a great deal of tension in his arms, shoulders, and neck. The tensed or "tied-up" 440 man is very easy to recognize at the end of a race—his arms display a rough, jerky motion; his chin is held high with head back; and strain shows in all parts of his body.

Summary

The principles of starting and sprinting form are essentially the same in all events up to the 440-yard dash. Although potential for sprinting speed is mostly an inherited talent, an athlete can improve his speed through diligent training and attention to details. A person can improve his speed in two ways—by conditioning and by attention to details of sprinting technique. Always striving to go "all-out" under control is the best means of attaining peak performance in sprinting.

2

Relay Racing

The climax to nearly every track and field meet is the mile relay. Part of the excitement of this event undoubtedly stems from the fact that it is often the deciding factor in a track meet. Perhaps, however, the real excitement comes from seeing a blending of the effort of the fatigued athlete with that of a fresh runner. This blending of effort is demonstrated in the baton exchange. Although a team may not have the four fastest runners on the track, it may have the best baton passes and, as a result, win the race; it is the team which gets the baton from the starting line to the finish line first that wins!

There are a variety of relays which can be run, and all of them involve four runners. There are the *sprint relays*—four by 110 yards, four by 220 yards, and four by 440 yards; the *distance relays*—four by 880 yards and four by one mile; and the *medley relays*—sprint medley (440, 220, 220, and 880), distance medley (440, 880, three-quarter mile, and one mile), and high school medley (110, 220, 440, and 880 yards).

Exchanges

The exchange zone is twenty meters in length, and all exchanges must occur within this zone. In sprint relays, the outgoing runner may start from a point ten meters behind the exchange zone.

Types of Exchanges

There are two basic types of exchanges—*visual* (open) and *non-visual* (closed or blind). Visual exchanges, in which the outgoing runner keeps visual contact with the incoming runner, are used for distance relays and for novice runners. Nonvisual exchanges are used in the sprint relays. The mile relay appears to be the cross-

8

over point between the use of nonvisual and visual exchanges; that is, most mile relay passes will be visual, but as a team works together and becomes more proficient, they may progress to a nonvisual exchange.

Regardless of the type of relay, there must be a coordination of the efforts of the incoming runner and the outgoing runner. This coordination of effort comes about with the aid of a *checkpoint*, or marker, on the track. As the incoming runner passes this point, the outgoing runner begins to run, always taking at least three strides before preparing to accept the baton. In other words, the outgoing runner concentrates initially solely on getting started. Obviously, the faster the incoming runner is moving, the farther away the checkpoint should be. In sprint relays, the checkpoint may be as much as seven to nine yards from the outgoing runner. In distance relays, it will be about three to five yards from the outgoing runner. Figure 2.1 illustrates the relationship between the speeds of the two runners. Because he is approaching fatigue, the incoming runner will be slowing down. At the same time, the outgoing runner is accelerating rapidly. Thus, the race becomes a matter of coordinating the speeds of the two runners.

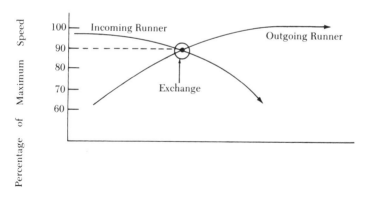

FIGURE 2.1. *Relationship between Speeds of Two Runners*

Nonvisual Exchanges. When the nonvisual exchange is used, the responsibility for the pass belongs with the incoming runner because it is he who must get to the outgoing runner and put the baton in his outstretched hand. There are basically three kinds of nonvisual exchanges (see Figures 2.2-2.4). The first is a *palm-upward, arm-rotated-outward exchange*. With this exchange, the incoming runner must bring the baton *downward* into the outgoing runner's hand. The second type is the *palm-upward, arm-rotated-inward exchange*. Again, the incoming runner must bring the baton *downward* into the outgoing runner's hand. The third technique is a *palm-down, thumb-in method* in which the incoming runner must place the baton with an *upward* motion. It cannot be emphasized enough that the incoming runner must *slap* the baton into the outgoing runner's hand.

The baton is coming down into the hand of the outgoing runner.

FIGURE 2.2. *Palm-upward, Arm-Rotated-outward Nonvisual Exchange*

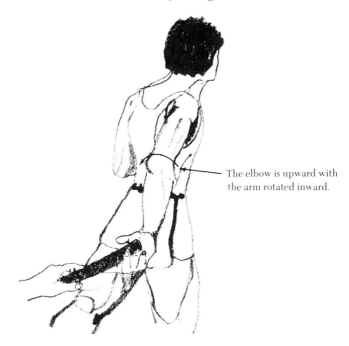

The elbow is upward with the arm rotated inward.

FIGURE 2.3. *Palm-upward, Arm-Rotated-inward Nonvisual Exchange*

The first two of these techniques are adapted particularly to a relay in which the runners do not switch the baton from one hand to the other. For example, the first runner, who might have the baton in his **right** hand, gives it to the second runner who accepts and keeps the baton in his **left** hand. The second runner hands to the third runner who accepts and keeps the baton in his *right* hand. The fourth runner will receive the baton in his *left* hand. The third technique mentioned requires the runner to switch the baton to the opposite hand from that in which he received it (see Figure 2.4). Thus, all passes will be from right hand to left hand or vice versa when using this method.

Visual Exchanges. As was mentioned earlier, visual exchanges are used in distance relays. Since the outgoing runner has visual contact with the incoming man when using this exchange, he has the responsibility of "taking" the baton from the incoming runner.

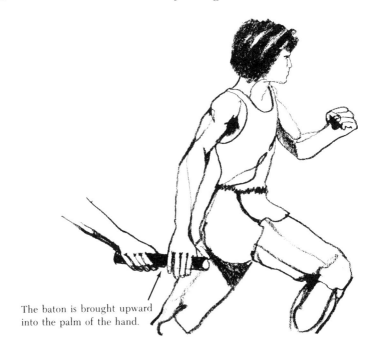

The baton is brought upward
into the palm of the hand.

FIGURE 2.4.   *Palm-down, Thumb-in Nonvisual Exchange*

One of the more popular techniques for visual exchange is to
have the palm placed upward and the arm rotated outward (see Figure 2.5). The receiver keeps his eyes on the incoming runner *after*
an initial three-step accelerating drive down the track. *Then,* he
looks back over the receiving hand for the baton.

A second technique is to form a "gunsight" with a "v" formed
by the thumb and fingers of the hand. The palm of the hand is facing
the incoming runner (see Figure 2.6). This technique gives the
runner a larger target at which to aim. The outgoing runner again
has the responsibility of "taking" the baton from his mate.

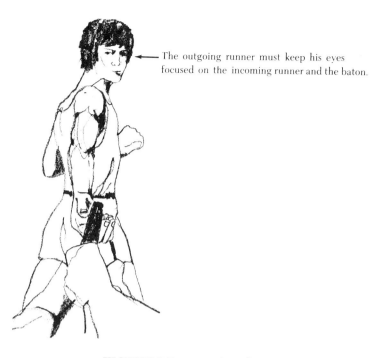

The outgoing runner must keep his eyes focused on the incoming runner and the baton.

FIGURE 2.5. *Visual Exchange*

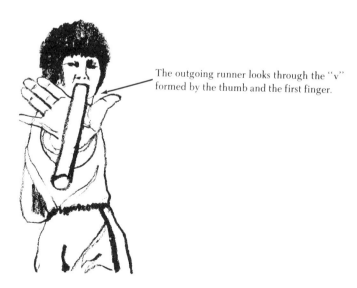

The outgoing runner looks through the "v" formed by the thumb and the first finger.

FIGURE 2.6. *"Gunsight" Technique of Exchange*

3

Hurdles

With the elimination of the 220-yard low hurdle event from collegiate competition in the early 1960s, hurdling was taken out of the realm of the sprinter and placed in the hands of the hurdling specialist. At the same time that the 220-yard low hurdles were eliminated, the 330- and 440-yard intermediate hurdles were added to the collegiate schedule of events. Now the 440-yard intermediates are favored almost universally over the 330-yard intermediate hurdle event; however, high schools do still use the 180-yard low hurdle event. A low hurdle event of either 120 or 180 yards is appropriate for a physical education setting.

The standard heights of the hurdles are: collegiate and international high hurdles, forty-two inches; collegiate intermediate hurdles thirty-six inches; high-school high hurdles, thirty-nine inches; high-school low hurdles, thirty inches. See Table 3.1 for the details of each of the hurdling events.

Essentials Of Hurdling

Getting Started

The essentials of good starting and sprinting technique also apply to the hurdles. The hurdler should have sufficient speed so that he could fit into a sprint relay team or even substitute for a sprinter in the 100- or 220-yard dash. Unlike athletes in other running events, the hurdler has to learn to control his strides leading up to the first hurdle and between each hurdle. Learning to hurdle requires the patience to begin with simple actions and stay with them until each is mastered and, finally, integrated into the whole action.

"Driving over" the Hurdle

For learning purposes, setting the hurdle at a height of thirty-six inches (intermediate-hurdle height) is quite useful after intro-

14

TABLE 3.1

*Dimensions and Distances of
the Various Hurdle Events*

Event	Hurdle Height	Distance to First Hurdle	Number of Hurdles	Distance between Hurdles	Distance from Last Hurdle to Finish
120-yard high hurdles (college)	3 feet, 6 inches	15 yards	10	10 yards	15 yards
110-meter hurdles	107 centimeters	13.72 meters	10	9.14 meters	14.02 meters
180-yard low hurdles	2 feet, 6 inches	20 yards	8	20 yards	20 yards
440-yard intermediate hurdles	36 inches	49.21 yards	10	38.27 yards	46.5 yards
400-meter intermediate hurdles	91.4 centimeters	45 meters	10	35 meters	40 meters

ductory work has been completed. Although different coaches describe how one approaches the problem of getting over the barrier, the movement is rarely described as "popping over" or "jumping over." It is most often described as *attacking, driving over,* or *skimming over* the hurdle. The idea is to drive over the hurdle, keeping the center of gravity in the line of running as much as possible and spending a minimum of time in flight over the barriers (see Figure 3.1).

"Lift," "Kick," "Snap." With only slight modifications, the hurdler tries to maintain a sprinting profile. The lead leg (preferably the left) follows the pattern of a lift with the left knee, followed by a kicking, or straightening action of the lower leg, then snapping down of the entire leg. The sequence can be thought of as *lift, kick, snap.* Practice this sequence by first just standing on the track

FIGURE 3.1. *Completed Form*

16

and slowly "lifting" the knee, "kicking" the lower leg, and "snapping" the entire leg back to the track. Go *easy* at first and gradually increase the cadence. When a consistent rhythm has been achieved, it is time to start thinking of the arms.

Arm Action. Some coaches think in terms of thrusting both arms forward toward the foot of the lead leg thus actually simulating a "dive" over the hurdle. If one can learn to control arm motion to the extent that he can maintain an arm-leg opposition pattern as in running, he will be more efficient in getting over the barrier. The primary function of arm action is to counteract the rotating tendency of the trunk (see Figure 2.2). That is, the lead leg is lifted in clearing the hurdle, the body tends to rotate around its vertical axis. Thus, an exaggerated action of the *opposite* arm is required to keep the athlete in a straight line of action. If the *left* leg is acting as the lead, the *right* arm must be extended or driven forward to the *left*

FIGURE 3.2. *Lift, Kick, Snap Drill*

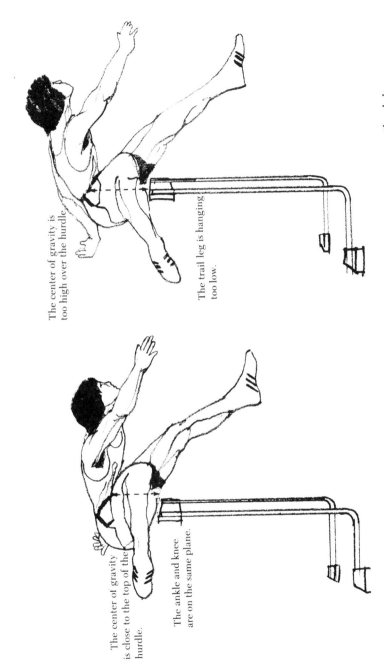

The center of gravity is
too high over the hurdle.

The trail leg is hanging
too low.

FIGURE 3.4. *Poor Flexibility*

The center of gravity
is close to the top of the
hurdle.

The ankle and knee
are on the same plane.

FIGURE 3.3. *Flexibility*

18

foot. This can be practiced by adding arm action to the "lift," "kick," "snap" drill. As the "kick" is executed, the opposite hand is "flicked" toward the lead foot. The arm on the *same* side as the lead leg is maintained close to the side and allowed to come forward *no farther* than the knee.

The Trail Leg.   The trail leg is the final consideration, since we have thus far been doing "land" drills. The trail leg must come over the hurdle with the knee and ankle in the same plane. This requires rotating the leg at the hip and lifting outward (abducting). Hip flexibility is very important to the hurdler. If his hip flexibility is such that he cannot lift and rotate the trail leg high enough, he will be forced to raise his center of gravity higher in order to clear the trail leg (see Figures 3.3 and 3.4). This, of course, is what the good hurdler avoids (i.e., raising the center of gravity very high and spending more time in flight).

From the Start to the Finish

The first hurdle is fifteen yards from the starting line in the high-hurdle event. For the beginner, this distance presents a problem because the natural starting position of his legs is such that he will arrive at the first hurdle leading with the "wrong" leg or arrive either too close to or too far away from the take-off point. Depending on leg limb length, stride length, and driving force, hurdlers will arrive at the first hurdle in seven, eight, or nine strides. Most hurdlers will be there in eight strides (see Figure 3.5). Note that in the eight-stride approach the position of the feet is opposite to that of the seven- or nine-stride approach.

Once the hurdler has landed after flight over the first hurdle, he will take three strides before flight over the second hurdle. This pattern will continue throughout the race. The achievement of balance between the hurdle and straight-ahead running becomes paramount in the achievement of a successful hurdle race. The principles of finishing are the same as those for a sprinter. For best results, one must sprint through the finish line.

Learning the Event

As with any other event, there are a variety of approaches to learning and practicing the fundamentals of the hurdling event.

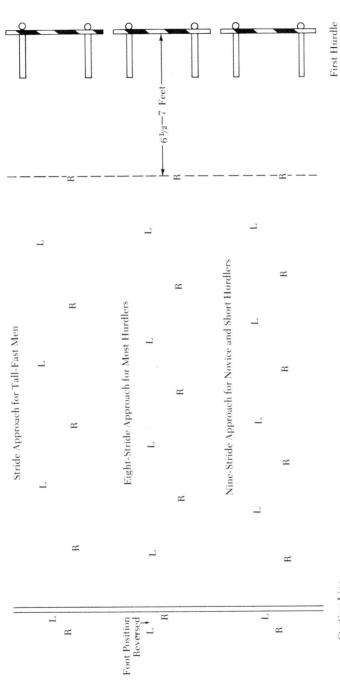

FIGURE 3.5. *Stride Pattern*

20

One of the most practical ways to start is to use the "lift," "kick," "snap" routine as described on pp. 115-19.

Spend several minutes for the first few sessions working on this technique. Arm action can be added the first day. As the rhythm becomes better, lean forward, bending at the hips, as the hand is thrust toward the opposite foot.

Set up low barriers (approximately one foot high) about ten yards apart using old vaulting crossbars or bamboo sticks. Don't worry about the number of steps between hurdles; just get used to lifting the lead leg a little higher as you go over each obstacle (see Figure 3.6). Eventually, try taking three steps between the hurdles. If you cannot do this, shorten the distance between hurdles to nine yards. Gradually, elevate the height of the barrier until low hurdle height is reached. From this point onward, all practice of hurdling should be over the actual hurdle. For advanced technique work, hurdles should be placed at a racing height.

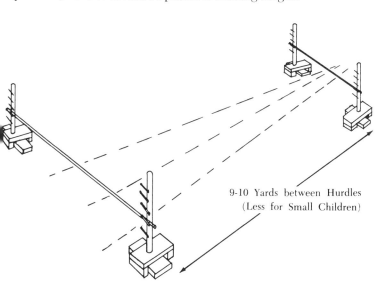

9-10 Yards between Hurdles
(Less for Small Children)

FIGURE 3.6. *Set-up for Teaching Beginners*

A great deal of learning and refinement can be accomplished by practicing first with one flight of hurdles, then two, then three. Specific objectives must be kept in mind as each variety of flight numbers is tried. For example, a hurdler might be attempting to improve his start and drive over the first hurdle. Another objective might be to maintain balance and drive over the first and second hurdles.

The 440-Yard Intermediate Hurdles

The requirements for the intermediate hurdles are slightly different than those for the other hurdle events because this race involves a combination of speed, endurance, and stride plan. The last two or three hurdles can seem to be a great deal higher than three feet for the hurdler who has gone too fast during the first half of the race. It can be debated whether a good 440 runner who adapts to hurdling technique or a good hurdler with endurance makes the better intermediate man. I am inclined to think that the 440 runner has an advantage with his experience at running the distance, for the runner in the event has to have the ability to judge pace and distribute his energy over the entire race.

Earlier, it was suggested that the student learn hurdling technique with a left-leg lead. Whenever one runs a curve over hurdles (as in the 440-yard intermediate hurdles), there is a slight advantage for the man who leads with the inside leg (left leg). If he leads with the right leg, he is actually driving his body *away from* the line of action. Also, he is forced to run a slightly wider arc than the athlete with the left leg lead.

4

Middle-Distance and Distance Running

The *middle-distance* races include events of distance greater than 440 yards and less than two miles or 5000 meters. Races of length beyond this arbitrary point are classified as *distance* events, with *long distances* including the marathon (twenty-six miles, 385 yards) and double marathon.

There is a great deal of folklore mixed in with scientific fact concerning distance running. The history of distance running is packed with emotional stories of superhuman efforts. The feats of Paavo Nurmi, Gundar Haegg, Emil Zatopek, Vladimer Kuts, Ron Clarke, Jim Ryun, Derek Clayton, and Ron Hill are indeed legend. But the future of distance running is even more promising than its past is illustrious. Can a man run a mile in 3:40? The answer is a resounding, "Yes"! Looking at Jim Ryun's world record time of 3:51.1 for the mile, we can see possibilities of a faster race. A basic physiological fact is that the most economical way to run is to maintain a steady pace throughout. In Ryun's tremendous effort, the splits for each quarter were 57.8 seconds, 57.5 seconds, 59.8 seconds, and 56.0 seconds. The first two quarters were remarkably close in pace, while the speed for the third quarter was 2.2 seconds slower. The final quarter was almost four seconds faster than the third. Even if Ryun had run 57.0 for the third and fourth quarters, he would have broken 3:50. Although it is not the purpose here to detract from Jim Ryun's outstanding performance, it is clearly evident from this example how little change has to be made to improve records in the distance events. To run the 3:40 mile, an average of fifty-five seconds per quarter would be required. Considering the fact that some miles have been run with a last quarter speed of under fifty-four seconds it is quite reasonable to contend that the right man could carry fifty-five-second quarters.

23

Form for Distance Running

Sprinting is done with the feet contacting the ground on the forward part of the ball of the foot. As the distance increases (and the pace becomes slower), the runner contacts the ground farther back on the ball of his foot. Long-distance form gives way to individual styles of hitting the ground with the foot flat or landing on the outside of the foot and rolling up onto the ball. Knee follow-through (commonly called leg lift) is not as great with progressive increases in distance. Basically, what occurs is a gradual change from sprinting to striding, and as the distance increases, efficiency in striding becomes paramount.

The profile of a middle-distance runner should show the individual to have an erect posture. Forward lean is not at all efficient. Donald Slocum,[1] an orthopedic surgeon, has demonstrated that the skeletal structure is so arranged that leg extension (hyperextension) at the hip joint is improved when the pelvic girdle is stabilized, the spinal column upright, and the chest high (see Figure 4.1).

In this position, one is able to attain greater driving force with hyperextension at the hip joint. It should be pointed out that forward lean should not be taught at this point. One does not lean forward *in order to* run faster but has a forward leaning profile *because* he is running faster (sprinting).

Achievement of the paradox of being relaxed while driving must be an objective which is blended into a smoothly coordinated individual style. Improvement in style comes about only through practice and more practice. The development of individual style often appears to be secondary in a training program but can be just as important as the training objectives of speed and endurance.

Training For Distance Running

When considering training, a coach should look at the needs of an individual for a particular distance. Since the two primary ingredients in running are speed and endurance, we can say, even at the risk of oversimplification, that as the distance increases, the

[1]Donald B. Slocum and W. Bowerman, "The Biomechanics of Running," *Clin Orthop.* 23 (1962): 39-45.

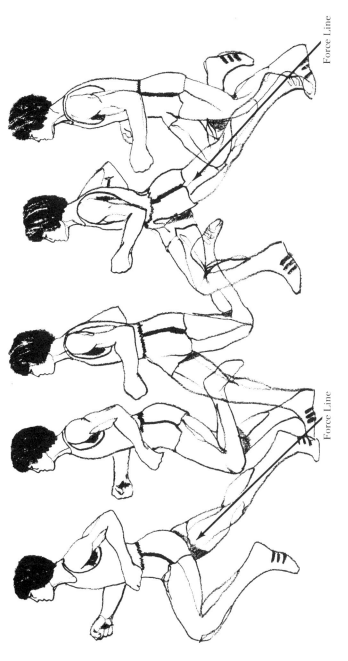

Force Line

Force Line

FIGURE 4.1. *Profile of the Middle-Distance Runner*

need for speed is reduced and the need for endurance, or lasting power, is increased. Nonetheless, in saying that the need for speed is reduced, it should not be assumed that it is no longer important. The ability to carry a fast last quarter is a bonus that all distance runners desire.

In any training system, one of the key components is the volume of running, or total distance covered. Provision also should be made to increase the *intensity* of work over a competitive season. Although volume is more important in the early stages of a competitive season, intensity becomes important toward the end of competitive season. Another way to state this concept is to say that there is a change in emphasis from quantity to quality of training (see Figure 4.2).

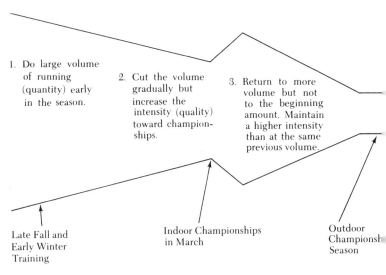

1. Do large volume of running (quantity) early in the season.

2. Cut the volume gradually but increase the intensity (quality) toward championships.

3. Return to more volume but not to the beginning amount. Maintain a higher intensity than at the same previous volume.

Late Fall and Early Winter Training

Indoor Championships in March

Outdoor Championship Season

FIGURE 4.2. *Training for Distance Running*

Interval Training

For every champion runner there is an individual approach to training. One of the more popular training systems in the United States is *interval training*. In this system, a fraction of the racing distance (usually one-quarter or one-eighth of the distance) is used as the training distance. In its original form, as projected by Woldemar Gerschler, the basic distance of interval training was 200 meters. Within this frame, several components may be altered, including the rate (or intensity) of running, the number of repetitions, and the time for rest between repetitions. The intensity can be altered by increasing the rate of running and by decreasing the time for rest between runs. Within these limits, there is a great deal of variation dependent upon individual tolerance, strengths, and weaknesses.

How much volume should an individual runner aim for in a workout? There is no set answer to this question for the answer is partly dependent upon the competitive distance in the individual athlete's event and the time of season. The volume can range all the way from fifteen times racing distance down to twice the racing distance. In addition, it should be noted that from time to time during the competitive season, a complete change of routine is desirable. For example, going from a routine of twenty times 440 yards in seventy seconds to a long cross-country run may be desirable. It is important for the athlete to get away from the 440-yard oval on occasion. Often, as a runner matures, he spends less time on the track and more time running cross-country courses along rivers and in woods.

This type of "escape" running preceded the development of interval training as a system and even has a name. Developed in Sweden, it is called *fartlek*, or *speed-play*. While on the surface *fartlek* appears to be a low-pressure, easy form of training, it is, in fact, very demanding. One has to be well disciplined to force himself to undergo the tempo changes that occur during a one-hour *fartlek* run. Being able to charge up a hill at an all-out speed, then do a slow jog for several hundred yards, then pick up the tempo for 800 yards or so, and, finally, do a series of sprints and jogs is a very real challenge.

The objective of *fartlek* training is to have the athlete undergo a training stimulus without the usual drudgery and boredom of working on the track. It is a system that developed *naturally* in the Scandinavian countries, for with the beautiful countryside, pine forests, and varieties of terrain, nothing could be a more natural, exhilarating, and challenging method than to train in this environment!

Marathon Running

Although every event has its moment of truth, marathon running can have the longest and most painful of these moments. The ability to sustain oneself over a distance of twenty-six miles, 385 yards is indeed a special quality. There is a unique tenacity and dedication that is required of those seeking to be among the members of the marathon-finishers club. Whether one can run the marathon in two hours, twenty minutes or four hours is not really important; being able to say with a certain pride that one *finished* a marathon is important.

One of the advantages of the marathon is that one does not have to be blessed with speed to participate in it. The race is primarily one of endurance. A runner who can run a mile in only 4:30 may be able to train himself sufficiently to maintain a 5:30 mile pace for the marathon. This would result in a very respectable time of two hours, twenty-five minutes.

Preparation for the Marathon

One doesn't decide that he is going to be a marathoner one day and go out the next day and run a race. Becoming a marathon runner probably is a process of evolution that takes place over several years. Although it is possible for a person to train for the event without ever having been a distance runner, marathoners are most often athletes who have run the middle distances and moved up gradually to races of greater length.

An athlete may spend a year in preparation for his first marathon race. The training process is one of gradually increasing mileage covered up to a point of approximately 100 miles per week. Some good marathoners can log between 800 and 900 miles per month. Periodic test races of six, ten, fifteen, and even twenty miles are necessary precursors to running the full marathon. Regardless of one's achievement as a marathon runner, there is a satisfaction in knowing one's capabilities and in meeting a challenge. The challenge is not unlike that of mountain climbing. Regardless of preparation, the first attempt at a competitive marathon undoubtedly will be disappointing. "Buddy" Edelen, America's premier marathoner in the early 1960s, has said that becoming a good marathoner involves gaining experience by running several marathon races. The novice marathoner should not be surprised if he finishes his first competitive effort in a time of between three and four hours. The important point is that he was able to finish!

Jogging

When one doesn't have the time or inclination to become a competitive marathoner, a very good substitute is the activity of jogging. The word "jogging" itself implies a slow-pace run which is slightly faster than a walk (at about five to six miles per hour, one has to break into a jog). Jogging is an excellent activity for the person who feels the need for exercise yet does not want to become involved in great expenditures for sports equipment or exercise sessions at the local health spa. Primarily, all the prospective jogger needs is a medical examination and a pair of lightweight canvas shoes. It is most essential that a person obtain the go-ahead of his physician. After this, training becomes a matter of *gradual* exposure to jogging.

There have been reports in national news magazines which give an unfavorable impression of the medical consequences of jogging because a few individuals either *started too ambitiously* or were neither prepared nor medically fit for *any* type of strenuous activity. The careless manner of handling reports of deaths by the press has unfairly implicated jogging as the sole reason for the fatalities. One particular instance involved a person who had collapsed while exercising on one occasion and collapsed and died a few weeks later. The news media simply reported that the person died while jogging. What it failed to report was that the victim had been on a severe diet, had lost forty pounds in a period of three to four months, and was hypoglycemic at the time of death. The point is that even before the first collapse, the man should have been working closely with a physician familiar with sports medicine. At the very least, he should have consulted his physician following the first collapse and stopped exercising until the cause of collapse was diagnosed and remedied!

What to Wear

The most comfortable attire for jogging includes a pair of running shorts, t-shirt, and rubber-soled running shoes. One can substitute a pair of khaki trousers for running shorts. As the weather gets cooler (between thirty-five and fifty degrees), the addition of a sweat shirt is appropriate. It is not necessary to wear a complete sweat suit at this time because the body generates enough heat to keep the runner warm. However, if these temperatures cause discomfort, then a sweat suit or khaki pants and sweat shirt could be added. In colder weather, two sweat shirts or sweat shirt and windbreaker will do nicely. A pair of inexpensive cloth gloves and a skier's ear tabs will suffice as additional equipment. It is not advisable for the jogger to wear a sweat suit in warm weather (above sixty degrees) because of the posibility of heat stress. Wearing a sweat suit or rubberized suit in warm weather in order to lose weight shows only that the person does not understand weight control. Most of the weight lost at this time is simply water and will be replaced in the several hours following exercise.

Thoughts about Starting the Jogging Program

A few years ago, President Kennedy suggested that the people of the United States should be capable of completing a fifty-mile hike. As a result, many dignitaries and groups of individuals initiated fifty-mile hikes. The number who were able to complete the distance was very small compared with the number who started. The reason for this was the lack of preparation; before one can walk fifty miles, he has to be able to walk one, ten, fifteen, twenty, or thirty miles. The point is that even for such a mild activity as walking, precautions must be taken before a program is undertaken.

Starting a planned exercise program, such as jogging, requires de termination and persistence to carry through with plans. The firs three or four weeks of a new program can be very discouraging Muscles will be sore; distances will be short; and results will be meager. But one fact should remain firm in the mind of the begin ner; *as the human body is exposed to exercise, it improves in response to the exercise stimulus.*

The beginning jogger should follow two very good guidelines for speed control: he should not be running so fast that his breathing is labored or that he has a feeling of "air hunger" (i.e. the feeling that he is gasping for air); his heart rate should not exceed a rate of 160 to 170 beats per minute. Respiratory rate and depth will natur ally be increased with exercise; nonetheless, this can occur without making the runner uncomfortable. Later in the jogging program this breathing guideline will be changed somewhat as new challenge re presented. After a period of several weeks, the jogger will be ble to feel comfortable while breathing more heavily and running at a aster rate.

The heart rate response referred to above is the immediately post-exercise heart rate counted within fifteen to thirty seconds after exercise. Usually, a jogger counts his heart beat for fifteen seconds, hen multiplies this figure by four to obtain a rate for one minute. here are two areas that can be palpated easily for counting rates. he first is on the thumb (radial) side of the wrist on the anterior palm) aspect; this is called the *radial pulse*. The second, which s very easy to locate after exercise, is on the neck just below the ngle of the jawbone; this is called the *carotid pulse*. In palpating, it s best to apply light pressure to either area using the first two fing-rs of the hand (see Figures 4.3 and 4.4).

Program Design

Before starting a jogging program, it is important to realize that here is no short cut to fitness. As a participant in a physical-fitness rogram, one should think of year-round involvement on a basis of articipation at least every other day. It is the purpose of the present iscussion to prepare the individual to be able to run between three nd ten miles continuously.

Exactly what distance a person should run is a difficult thing to nticipate because each of us has needs which are unique and each f us responds uniquely to exercise. To set a goal, one should re-member that the jogging session should be of at least fifteen minutes uration and can eventually go on for as much as an hour. It is vigor-usly recommended that the exercise session not be longer than fteen to twenty minutes when one is beginning a program! The type f jogging should be very slow in nature (a ten to fourteen minute ile pace). After the first mile, the jogger should walk for two or hree minutes (this is a good time to check the pulse rate), and hen finish the session by doing some more easy jogging. Another pproach is to jog short distances of 200 to 400 yards at a slightly fast-r pace and then walk for a like distance checking the pulse rate fter each running bout to determine whether the pace should be aster or slower. It is highly recommended that this latter approach e taken at first so that the jogger can monitor his heart rate and radually adjust to the exercise program.

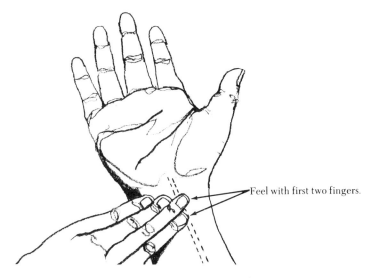

Feel with first two fingers.

FIGURE 4.3. *Radial Pulse*

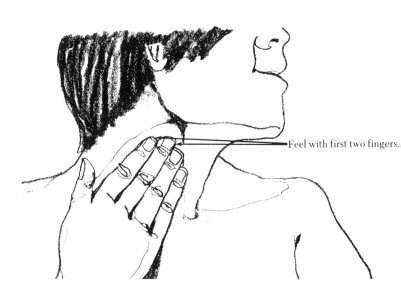

Feel with first two fingers.

FIGURE 4.4. *Carotid Pulse*

A typical jogging sequence to follow can be found in Table 4.1.

The objective of the series of seven phases in Table 4.1 is to improve endurance to a point where the jogger is able to cover two miles walking and jogging. At the end of each 200-250-yard jogging sector, the pulse should be counted. If the pulse rises above 170 beats per minute after any repetition, two adjustments can be made. First, a longer rest can be taken between repetitions (thus letting the heart rate return to approximately 120 beats per minute). Second, the speed of jogging can be slowed. Although in effect, the *rate* of work is being reduced, the exercise physiologist might state that the *intensity* of work is being reduced. Intensity is the key to improving the individual's physical fitness.

TABLE 4.1

| | Jog | | Walk | | Number of Repitions |
Phase	Distance	Time	Distance	Time	
1	200-250 yards	:50-1:30	200 yards	3-4 minutes	4
2	200-250 yards	:50-1:30	200 yards	3-4 minutes	6
3	200-250 yards	:50-1:30	200 yards	3-4 minutes	8
4	200-250 yards	:50-1:30	200 yards	3-4 minutes	10
5	200-250 yards	:50-1:30	200 yards	3-4 minutes	12
6	200-250 yards	:50-1:30	200 yards	3-4 minutes	14
7	200-250 yards	:50-1:30	200 yards	3-4 minutes	16

After completion of these phases, there are several avenues of departure open for continuation of the jogging program. The one suggested below is favored by the author if a person is interested simply in jogging. The overall scheme is to set target times in which each distance is to be run. As an illustration, one might cite the jogger whose goal is 8:30 for one mile, 12:45 for 1½ miles, and 17:30 for two miles. The target time need not be accomplished on the first try, nor must the jogger run only that distance until he achieves the target time. The idea is to keep a log of distances covered and times achieved. There is no greater motivator than to see one's improvement over a period of weeks or months. One particular day's performance may be disappointing, but when put in the perspective of a week's performance, the overall picture will be one of accomplishment. As an example of a possible sequence of target times, the following table is provided.

TABLE 4.2

Run	Distance	Target Time	Actual Time	Target Rate	Actual Rate
1	1 mile	8:00	8:15	8:00	8:15
2	2 miles	16:30	17:20	8:15	8:40
3	1½ miles	12:15	12:30	8:07	8:30
4	1 mile	8:00	8:10	8:00	8:10
5	3 miles	25:30	27:00	8:30	9:00
6	1 mile	8:00	8:10	8:00	
7	2 miles	16:30		8:15	
8	1 mile	8:00	8:05	8:00	
9	1 mile	8:00	8:05	8:00	
10	4 miles	34.20	36:40	8:40	9:10
11	1 mile	8:00	8:00	8:00	
12	2 miles	16:30		8:15	
13	1 mile	8:00	8:00	8:15	
14	3 miles	25:30		8:30	
15	1 mile	8:00	8:00	8:00	
16	1 mile	8:00	8:00	8:00	
17	5 miles	43:45	48:00	8:45	9:36

An ultimate goal would be to run all of the target times. This can by a dynamic and flexible situation in that some target times will be achieved before others and thus new target times for those distances can be established. At the beginning of this section, it was indicated that there was no short cut to fitness and that part of the program would be difficult. Running three miles thirty seconds faster on a second or third time does take determination. The possibilities—even for a person with no previous athletic running experience—are unlimited. The author has known cases of individuals who have taken up jogging at the age of fifty and progressed to *running* ten miles in seventy-three minutes (7:20 per mile). There is another case of a man fifty-four years old who could run four miles in twenty-five minutes (6:15 per mile). These are examples of extreme cases of achievement; however, the average individual will not and does not need to run more than three to six miles during his peak of fitness.

More information on jogging and fitness can be acquired by reading a book entitled *Jogging* by William J. Bowerman and W.E. Harris.[2]   For a more detailed perspective on physical fitness programs, two books, *The New Aerobics* by Kenneth Cooper[3] and *Conditioning Fundamentals* by Edward Olson,[4] are recommended. A jogging program may not provide the complete answer to attaining physical fitness for everyone, but it does offer tremendous benefits for a wide variety of persons.

---

[2]William J. Bowerman and W. E. Harris, *Jogging* (New York; Grosset and Dunlap, Publishers, 1967).

[3]Kenneth H. Cooper, *The New Aerobics* (New York; Bantam Books, 1968).

[4]Edward Olson, *Conditioning Fundamentals* (Columbus, Ohio; Charles E. Merrill Publishing Co., 1967).

The Jumping Events

5

The High Jump

Of the two basic techniques of high jumping *the straddle* and *the western roll*, the straddle with its many modifications is more popular among today's high jumpers. Two other techniques, the *eastern cut-off* and *scissors*, had a certain popularity in the early days of high jumping but have since been shown to be much more inefficient than either the straddle or western roll. Efficiency in high jumping involves the position of the center of gravity as the body passes over the bar. When perfecting high-jumping technique, the prime objective is to have the center of gravity pass as close to the bar as possible or *under the bar!*

Elements of the Event

The Run-up or Approach

The approach is basically the same whether the jumper is using the western roll or straddle. By keeping in mind that transforming the horizontal velocity of the run to vertical velocity of the jump is essential, the jumper realizes that it is imperative to have a *fast, controlled* approach. The jumper who relies solely on natural leg spring and ignores the approach will have only limited success. It is a little more difficult to control the approach, when first learning, but the important thing to remember is to have a smooth approach while accelerating the first five steps and to keep a fast, smooth run during the last six strides. (*Note:* The number of strides will vary depending upon the individual athlete.)

The ultimate success in high jumping depends upon the first step! Although American athletes have enjoyed a great deal of success in the high jump, they could enjoy even more success with a better run-up. European and Russian jumpers literally attack the bar from their first steps.

Using Figure 5.1 as a guide, the reader can see that the runner takes two walking steps, hits a checkpoint, and then accelerates as he approaches the bar; he prepares to begin the block by leaning back between the ninth and tenth strides and *really* leaning back when the take-off foot hits the ground (on the eleventh step). He leans so much that the heel of the take-off foot hits the ground first. This action is known as the *block*.

The overall effect of the block is to halt or slow down forward momentum and cause an upward movement of the body. An analogy would be the lifting of the rear end of a car as it slams into a solid wall. The difference is that with the high jumper there is an additional contribution to upward movement; the lead leg and both arms are utilized in the jump.

The take-off leg is straight upon impact and flexes under the stress of momentum. It is very important to remember that the take-off foot should be planted well in front of the hips. As approach speed improves with practice, the take-off foot must be planted even farther in front of the hips. This whole process gives sufficient time for the lead leg and arms to contribute to the jump effort.

Western Roll

This technique entails hopping over the bar in a side lay-out position. It is one of the easiest jumping techniques to learn and may be used by young high jumpers. As the athlete matures, he will be challenged to try the straddle or belly-roll.

Selecting which leg he wants to use as the take-off leg is the first task. There are at least two ways of making this choice. The first involves simply standing in place and hopping on one foot. When someone says, "Start hopping," the athlete hops for a few seconds and stops. He then repeats the exercise. If he hops on the same leg both times, then that leg is probably his take-off leg. If, however, this exercise does not solve the problem, the athlete must try the second method. After placing the bar at two feet, six inches, the athlete approaches the bar at an angle, first from the right side, then from the left. He jumps over the bar any way he can. In so doing, he will either take off with the same leg on both tries or use one leg that

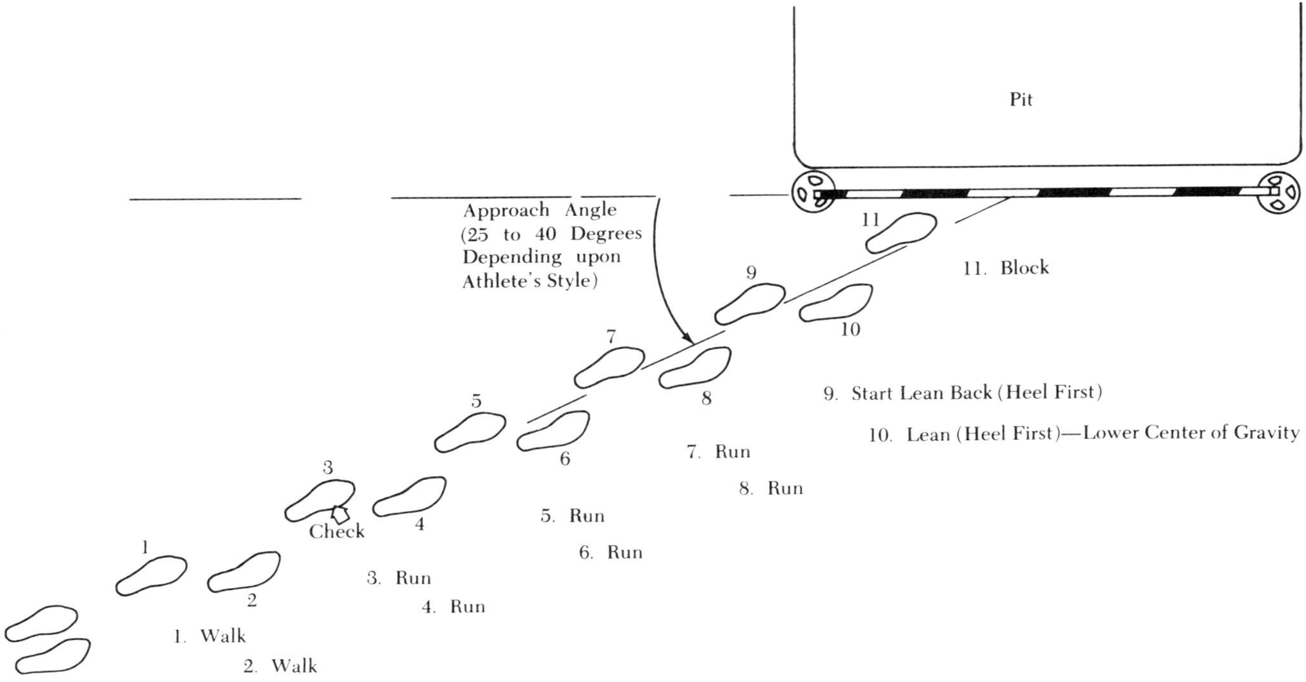
Pit
Approach Angle
(25 to 40 Degrees
Depending upon
Athlete's Style)
1
2
3
Check
4
5
6
7
8
9
10
11
1. Walk
2. Walk
3. Run
4. Run
5. Run
6. Run
7. Run
8. Run
9. Start Lean Back (Heel First)
10. Lean (Heel First)—Lower Center of Gravity
11. Block

FIGURE 5.1. *The Run-Up or Approach*

feels much better than the other. Most jumpers are left-footed and take-off on their left foot. This means that for both the western-roll and straddle-style jumpers, the approach will be made from the *left* side of the pit.

When going over the cross-bar, the jumper is in a side position; in other words, his *left* side is nearest the bar. The take-off leg has caught up to and is passing under the lead leg in a motion that looks almost as though the jumper were trying to tuck the jumping leg beneath his chin. If the arms are in proper position, the shoulders are in a rounded position with the forearms in front of the face. The head is turned downward (toward the left shoulder).

Postion over the Bar

Landing

Land on same leg as take-off.

FIGURE 5.2.   *The Western Roll*

The jumper makes what can be called a three-point landing with the two arms and the take-off leg. Thus, we see that the jumper has taken off and landed on the *same* leg. To facilitate the jump, the athlete should reach for the pit with both hands *only after he has cleared the bar*. To begin reaching downward before he has cleared the bar will cause his left shoulder to dip too low, thereby hitting the crossbar or limiting the jumper's height by raising his center of gravity too high.

Learning the Western Roll.   The easiest way to learn the western roll is to place a bar at a very low height (about two or 2.5 feet) and simply hop over the bar after running straight toward it. The next step is to change the approach angle so that the jumper is coming toward the bar at an angle of about forty-five degrees. Now the jumper is ready to do a lay-out over the bar in a semi-tuck position. In landing, the body should be parallel with the crossbar with the head pointing toward the left side.

Before the crossbar is moved to greater heights, the technique should be perfected so that it is very smooth at this low height. Then, the bar may be moved up six inch increments to about four feet; it then should be raised with smaller increments.

Straddle or Belly Roll

The straddle is really a very sophisticated jumping technique and requires a great amount of practice before perfection is achieved. The skill requires keeping the chest and body toward the bar throughout the jump. Thus, the jumper "rolls" around the bar. With a very efficient straddle, it is possible for the center of gravity of the jumper to pass through or even *beneath* the cross bar.

As the jumper leaves the ground, the lead leg is swung upwards starting with the knee joint in an extended position so that the leg is straight. The knee joint then flexes slightly as the jumper rocks over the take-off foot and starts upward. Both arms are driven upward with the right arm slightly more elevated than the left. After the jumper has left the ground, the lead leg, with the knee *bent*, is driven over the bar. The left arm is brought to a position close to the body with the hand placed near the stomach or chest. The right arm goes out and over the bar thus facilitating the rotational action. In a position over the bar, the head, the right arm, and right leg are on the pit side of the crossbar, while the left arm is along the side of the body and the left knee is bent. When the jumper begins his downward trajectory, the left knee and foot should be rotated upward and outward. (The jumper should assume a ''frog-leg'' position.) The jumper will land in the pit on his right side.

Learning the Straddle

If the beginner chooses to learn to high jump with the straddle, the jumper will work without a crossbar or pit. To get the feeling of the rotational motion, the jumper starts in a normal standing position and places his right foot to the left foot and points the toes of the right foot at an angle as close to 180 degrees from the direction of the toes of the left foot as he can. At this point, the jumper's weight is shifted from his left foot to his right foot. With the weight shift, the jumper lifts his left foot from the ground, rotating it counter-clockwise. While turning, the left knee and foot should be lifted and rotated outward so as to assume a ''frog-leg'' position.

Step two is to stand with the right foot twenty-four to thirty inches behind the left. Body weight should be on the right foot for the most part. This position simulates a preblocking position in which the hips and body are *behind* the blocking, or take-off leg. The jumper swings his right leg, right arm and shoulder, and the *whole* right side of his body up and around the left leg. He should land on his right foot at a point midway between the original foot positions, with the left knee and foot in an outward rotated position as before. Once this had been accomplished, the neophyte jumper may take a few strides (three or five) and repeat the jump to make sure that the *whole right side of his body goes up and around* his left side. However, since it is impossible to land at a point midway between the last two steps, the task now becomes one of landing as close to the take-off foot position as possible. After practicing this until he definitely has the feeling of rotating around the left side of the body with the *whole* right side of the body, the jumper is ready for the pit!

Training with the Pit

With the bar set at the soaring height of two feet, six inches, the jumper puts into action the technique he has been practicing. It is important to mention a word about approach angle at this time.

The technique described above may be used by athletes who use various approach angles. It works better, however, for the jumper who approaches from a fairly sharp angle (35 to 30 degrees). Although the jumper will "travel" some along the bar with this technique, "traveling" is not undesirable.

FIGURE 5.3. *Straddle Form over the Bar*

The Dobroth Modification of the Straddle

The Dobroth modification differs from the conventional straddle in two important respects. The first is that the approach angle is less than normal (approximately 27 degrees) and thus gives the jumper the feeling that he is approaching along the bar rather than running toward it. The second is that the jumper tries to get the lead leg into the pit as quickly as possible after getting the whole right side of the body over the bar. This differs from most straddle jumping techniques which emphasize a rigorous lead leg kick and lift, which get the lead leg as high as possible.

Summary

Regardless of the high jumping technique selected, the young athlete must keep in mind a few basic points. Leg strength, which is essential to explosive power in jumping, can be developed by a rigorous strength-building program with weights. The approach must be practiced to the point that it becomes "automatic." The young high jumper must have patience and analyze each jump, for the difference between success and failure is often no more than a fraction of an inch.

Basic Rules for the High Jump

1. The pit shall have a minimum width and depth of sixteen feet by twelve feet.

2. The high jump approach shall provide at least fifty feet of level, unvarying surface encompassing an arc of 180 degrees.

3. The vertical uprights or standards shall be at least twelve feet and not more than thirteen feet, 2.25 inches apart.

4. A legal jump is one in which a competitor jumps from one foot.

5. A missed jump is called then:
   a. The crossbar is displaced in an attempt to clear it.
   b. The jumper passes under the crossbar or touches the ground with any part of the body extended beyond the crossbar.
   c. The jumper approaches the crossbar and leaves the ground (other than when taking a warm-up approach).

6. A jumper is eliminated from competition when he has missed three consecutive times. This happens whether the misses occur at the same height or at a higher height.

6

The Long Jump and Triple Jump

The long jump and triple jump are similar in that both events require the athlete to take a long running approach to a "take-off" board which marks the beginning phase of each event. For the long jump, the rest of the execution is rather uncomplicated; the long jumper simply tries to jump as far as he can. However, in the triple jump, one must execute a "hop," a "step," and *then*, a "jump" after leaving the take-off board. Although an athlete who long jumps often triple jumps as well, competing in both events in championship competition becomes difficult because of the demands for complete concentration in each event. We will now make a serious examination of fundamentals of the long jump and then follow with a look at the triple jump.

The Long Jump

In the long jump the athlete must be concerned with elevating himself above the ground as well as traveling in a horizontal plane. Ideally, the take-off angle would be 45 degrees. But this ideal is never achieved because the athlete does not have enough leg strength to overcome his forward momentum. To achieve a take-off angle of 45 degrees, the athlete would have to make a very slow approach. If one could combine top sprinting speed of thirty-six to thirty-seven feet per second (about a 9.1-second hundred-yard dash) along with a four-foot elevation of the center of gravity, the athlete would be able to jump over thirty-six feet.[1] In practical terms, however, a long jumper rarely takes off at a speed exceeding thirty feet per second or elevates his center of gravity more than three to 3.5 feet.

---

[1] Geoffrey H.G. Dyson, *Mechanics of Athletics*, 4th ed. (London: University of London Press, 1967), p. 151.

Elements of the Event

Approach. Ideally, sprinters attain maximum horizontal velocity (running speed) after accelerating for 150 to 180 feet. For this reason, the question of how long the approach should be for the long jumper has a seemingly simple answer—150 to 180 feet. Yet it is a rare occurrence for a long jumper to start beyond 150 feet. A run of this length is not necessary for *most* athletes. As a matter of fact, a run of this length may become a detriment because as the runner's horizontal velocity becomes greater, leg strength must be developed to a higher level to elevate the center of gravity. Dyson[2] indicates that most world-class long jumpers approach the take-off board at about thirty feet per second (a speed equivalent to a ten-second hundred-yard dash).

To attain maximum *controllable* speed, a long jumper ordinarily should try for an approach of 120 feet (plus or minus fifteen feet). However, after several years of training, competition, and *study* of the event, the athlete would be doing himself a disservice by not trying to lengthen his run-up.

As he would in other field events in which an approach is required (high jump, pole vault, and triple jump), the long jumper should have a checkpoint located seven to nine strides from his starting point and no closer to the take-off board than about sixty feet. The checkpoint is a very valuable guide for the jumper, for it gives him a reference point to use during the approach. If he can accelerate at the same rate each time and step on the checkpoint without shortening or lengthening his strides, he will have a much better chance of hitting the take-off board properly. There is nothing more disappointing to a long jumper than to foul by an inch or to have a good jump with a take-off eighteen inches behind the board! If the jumper misses the checkpoint, he simply stops and starts over. This is much better than fouling at the take-off!

Take-off. The last two or three strides are included as a part of the take-off simply because the jumper begins his preparation for the jump at this point. There is a slight lowering of the center of gravity as the jumper prepares to land heel first on the take-off board. The jumper appears to "gather" as a result of lowering the center of

---

[2]*Ibid.*, p. 153.

gravity. The take-off leg must hit the board heel first in order to impart a significant vertical velocity (elevating force) to the jumper.[3] If he hits the take-off board with the ball of the foot (as in sprinting), his center of gravity will be too far forward and will pass over the take-off leg too rapidly. This will contribute to a *low* vertical velocity, and thus, the jump will be short and flat. Technically speaking, the jumper will have a tendency to rotate forward. He must hit the take-off board with a rocking "heel—foot—toe" action while keeping the chest high and driving the opposite leg upwards as if trying to take a step in the air. By keeping the chest high, the jumper actually is keeping his upper body in an erect posture.

FIGURE 6.1. *Take-off Position in the Long Jump*

---

[3]The combination of horizontal and vertical velocity determine take-off angle and trajectory.

Thus far, we have said nothing about the arms in long jumping. It would be a grave mistake to forget arm action in the jump. The "opposition" role of the arms is maintained at take-off. For example, if the left leg hits the take-off board and the right leg is driven upward, the left arm is also driven forward and upward. In an effort by the jumper to counteract leg action and forward rotation of the body, arm motion becomes a modified windmill type of action during the flight. All athletes will not have the same pattern of arm action during the flight and it would be a mistake to try to stereotype arm technique. The primary point about arm action is that it is a mostly natural phenomenon that occurs in an effort to compensate for actions by other parts of the body. At the finish of the jump, both arms come forward and down toward the feet, while at the instant of the impact of the heels on the pit, both arms are swung backwards vigorously in a fashion similar to a breaststroke maneuver in swimming.

Final Stage of Jump (Legs and Knees Elevated to Maintain Flight as Long as Possible)

Arms will swing vigorously backward in a manner similar to the movement of the breast stroker in swimming.

FIGURE 6.2.   *Landing in the Long Jump*

Flight. There are essentially two techniques of flight in the long jump, each of which has several variations. The first of these is described as the *hang* or *float technique*. With the hang, the jumper leaves the take-off board with his feet hanging below and behind him and his legs slightly bent at the knees. As the end of the jump nears, he pulls both legs up and simulates a jack-knife position for the landing.

FIGURE 6.3.   *The Float Position and Landing*

The second technique is referred to as the *hitch-kick*. It may be described as a "run-in-the-air." The jumper actually continues his running motion after he has lifted from the take-off board. With the hitch-kick, there are two stages of development. The first is for the jumper to learn to do the hitch-kick with one-and-one-half revolutions; then, after gaining a great deal of experience (several seasons of jumping), the jumper learns to do the hitch-kick with two-and-one-half revolutions. It becomes desirable to learn a two-and-one-half-turn hitch-kick not because the body position in the air has altered or been prolonged but because the feet have remained in the air longer.

FIGURE 6.4. *The Hitch-Kick*

Finish. The first parts of the body to hit the pit are the heels of both feet. Normally, the jumper does not have to worry about falling back toward the take-off board because his body has enough momentum to make him roll out over his feet. Just before his landing in the sand, the jumper will be reaching forward with both hands with his body in a jack-knife position. At the instant of impact, he will pull both of his arms back vigorously.

Learning the Event

As was stated earlier, the basic skill of long jumping, although it is very simple, can still be broken down into small units for concentrated practice. All elements of the event—take off, flight, and finish—can be practiced separately.

The take off can be practiced by taking a short approach (thirty to sixty feet) *without* concern for hitting the board. Points to concentrate on include slight lengthening of the last two or three strides and thus lowering the center of gravity; achieving a "heel-ball-toe" rocking action of the take-off foot; getting full extension of the take-off leg; and keeping the upper body erect as it "lifts" off the ground. This last technique is called a *pop-up*. It should be kept in mind that the idea is to be explosive but relaxed and to get as high in the air as possible.

Using the same pop-up technique, the jumper can work on the hitch-kick and landing. In working on the finish, the jumper concentrates on lifting the heels, reaching forward with them, and sitting down. The effectiveness of the pop-up as a practice technique can be great, for the athlete can concentrate on each of the stage of the event.

An excellent drill to use during practice of the long jump is a running pop-up exercise on the track. This exercise consists of repeating fifty- to 100-yard runs while doing a pop-up every four or five strides. The idea is to gain height while doing a hitch-kick. The athlete should land lightly on his feet and continue into the next part of the exercise. At first, he should repeat shorter distances, then proceed to distances up to 100 yards. The exercise should be repeated five to ten times during each practice in which it is used (see Figure 6.5).

The Triple Jump

The phrase "hop, step, jump" may at first seem to be a better descriptive expression than "triple jump" for this event. However, upon analysis, one realizes that the triple jump is just what its name implies, a series of three highly explosive jumps with certain restrictions. The needs of the triple jumper during take-off are slightly different from those of the long jumper, for the triple jumper must maintain a greater horizontal momentum. In other words, the jumper does not try to get as far as he can on the first phase of the triple jump (the "hop"), but he does try to go as far as he can and keep his balance for the second phase (the "step").

FIGURE 6.5. *Pop-up Drill*

10-12 FEET

53

Triple jumping is one of the more demanding activities in track and field. Many times the pride of young athletes has been bruised when upon trying the event, they find that their legs collapse under the tremendous pressures which are generated. The most universal difficulty that beginning triple jumpers have is achieving a good "step".

Elements of the Event

Approach and Take-Off. The approach of a triple jumper can be slightly longer than that of a long jumper because the angle of take-off for the "hop" phase does not have to be as great as that in the long jump. Although the objective of the triple jumper is to maintain a relatively high horizontal velocity while executing the "hop" and "step" phases of the jump, the other coaching points concerning approach and take-off are very similar to those described for the long jump and can be found on page 47.

From which foot should the jumper take off? Since both the "hop" and "step" phases are executed with the same foot, it is usually suggested that the stronger leg be used for the take-off. Thus, if an athlete leaves the take-off board with the right leg, he will land on the right leg to start the "step." As he comes down from the "step," he will land on the left leg and execute the final phase or "jump."

The "Hop." During childhood, each of us learned the hopping motion, which can be simply described as taking off and landing on the same foot. In the triple jump, as the jumper leaves the take-off board, his free leg is driven upward vigorously and rotated downward and backward as a half-hitch kick. As the athlete lands, the foot of the take-off leg is slapped vigorously onto the runway. At this point, his free leg should be behind the driving leg in preparation for another upward-forward lead. The arms play an opposition role during the "hop" and should remain close to the body.

Two of the common problems encountered while executing the "hop" phase are a hop which is too high and too long, thus usually resulting in a collapse of the landing leg (this error leads to a very short step) and a trajectory which is too low and usually results in a very short "hop." The first problem is caused by an unnecessarily large take-off angle, while the second is caused by a small take-off angle. Taking the analysis a step further, one can see that too large a take-off angle is caused by a blocking action similar to that required in the long jump. The low-trajectory "hop" is a result of the athlete's hitting the take-off board with his center of gravity nearly over or in front of the base of support.

The "Step."   If the "hop" has been achieved with good mechanics, the "step" begins with the contact foot flat on the runway, the free leg behind and driving forward, and the arms in the normal opposition position. As the free leg is driven forward and upward, the hands of both arms also are driven forward and upward before again assuming the opposition position. The lead knee is held high, near the athlete, while the driving leg trails. This position is held as the jumper "floats" and is maintained until he starts to descend. As the jumper nears the runway, his free leg (lead) is driven vigorously into the ground in a stomping fashion.

The most common fault in the "step" is not driving the lead knee upward toward the chest. This happens because the natural tendency is for the jumper to reach toward the ground with his lead leg. One has to fight this natural tendency to "reach" for the ground.

The "Jump."   The "jump" phase may be executed by using the same technique as a long jump. With what momentum he has left, the jumper must try to gain as much elevation as he can. Most triple jumpers use a "float" during this phase, but with practice, a hitch-kick could be used in place of the "float." The technique of landing is the same as that in the long jump. The elements of the triple jump are shown in Figures 6.6, 6.7, and 6.8.

Learning the Event

Two of the most critical components in learning the triple jump are the development of jumping rhythm and establishing a good "step." All beginners in the triple jump would do well to work on developing the feeling of a rhythmic "hop," "step," "jump" in a "one," "two," "three" pattern. Often the pattern is "one," "and two," "three." This arrhythmic pattern indicates a very short "step." A standard technique for practicing rhythm is to mark off an area on the track or, preferably, on the grass into evenly spaced distances. At first, these distances should be short (about three feet), but

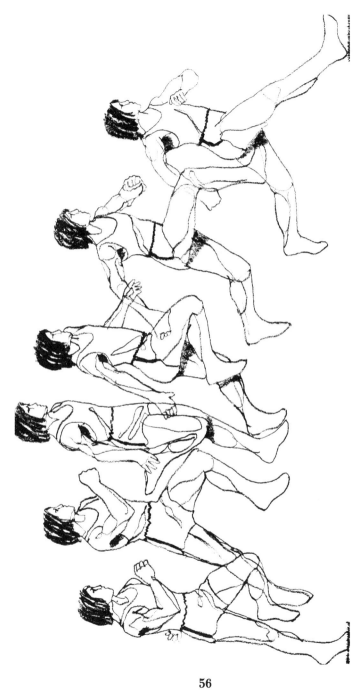

FIGURE 6.6. *The Hop*

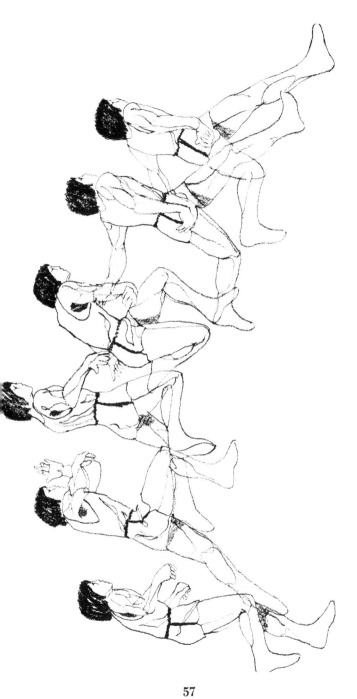

FIGURE 6.7. *The Step*

57

FIGURE 6.8. *The Jump*

58

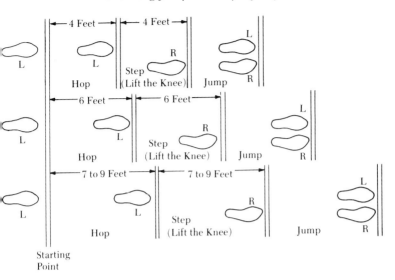

FIGURE 6.9.   *Layout for Practicing Rhythm in the Triple Jump*

they should be stretched later to about ten feet (see Figure 6.9).

By breaking the event down into its component parts, the jumper can practice the "hop" by simply hopping for short distances. At first, the distance should be about twenty-five yards, but gradually it can be worked up to several sets of seventy-five to 100 yards. Two types of "hops" can and should be practiced. The first is a relatively high springy "hop" in which the athlete experiences a rather hard landing. The second is called a "speed hop" in which the "hop" is rather flat. The idea of the second type is to acquaint the athlete with a fast turnover rate.

As was indicated earlier, the "step" is the key to a successful performance. A drill similar to the hopping drill can be utilized in perfecting the "step." But in this case, both legs are utilized in the drill. Emphasis is placed on lifting and holding the free knee near the chest (see Figure 6.10).

Practice of the "jump" phase can be the same as that in the long jump. For most practice situations, it would be desirable for the athlete to work either on grass or on one of the artificial surfaces currently available.

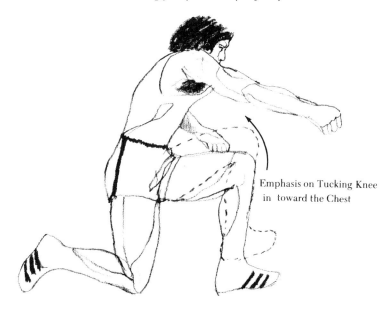

Emphasis on Tucking Knee
in toward the Chest

FIGURE 6.10.   *Step Drill*

Basic Rules for the Long Jump and Triple Jump

1. The take-off board for both the long and triple jumps shall be a wooden board, the upper surface of which is exactly level with the run-up surface.

2. The edge of the board nearest the pit shall be the foul line.

3. In the triple jump, the near edge of the landing pit shall be at least thirty feet from the take-off foul line. (*Note:* For physical education classes, it is advisable that the edge be not more than twenty-five feet from the scratch line.)

4. In the triple jump, the athlete must make his first jump (the "hop") by landing on the same foot from which he left the take-off board; his second jump (the "step"), by landing on the opposite foot from which he took off; and his third, by landing as he prefers.

5. Each legal jump shall be measured at right angles to the scratch

line from the nearest break in the ground, inside the landing pit, made by any part of the competitor's feet, hands, arms, body, or clothing to the scratch line extended.

6. A foul jump shall be said to occur in any of the following situations:

   a. If, during the take-off, the competitor's shoe extends over and beyond the scratch line.

   b. If, by attempting a jump, the athlete runs beyond the scratch line extended.

   c. If, during a jump, one foot drags the ground.

   d. If, while landing, the athlete touches the ground outside the landing pit closer to the take-off than where he landed in the pit.

7

The Pole Vault

In the integration of skills it requires, pole vaulting is, with little challenge from other events, the most demanding event in track and field. It demands a combination of speed, strength, endurance, and coordination that is not called for in any other single event. This is not to say that the pole vaulter is the strongest, fastest, most enduring, or most coordinated man on the track team, but he must possess a high degree of each of these qualities if he is to succeed in his event.

The pole vault, as are most other events, is a smoothly integrated sequence of movements. Although we see the event as a continuous series of actions, each of which is built upon the preceding action, it can be broken down into several components for analysis and learning. The phases of the vault can be described as the *run and approach, the plant, take-off, swing* (early and late phases), and *finish* (pull, turn, push). Different writers will give somewhat different descriptions of the breakdown of the event, but the preceding divisions are generally accepted.

Elements of the Event

The Run and Approach

As he would in other events involving a *run and approach*, the vaulter seeks to attain all-out speed *under control*. Although he has the problem of carrying the vaulting pole, the vaulter generally can achieve the desired speed by running from about 110 feet to 135 feet; some vaulters though will run as far as 150 feet or as little as eighty-five to ninety feet. To help him, the good vaulter usually will have a checkpoint either seven or nine strides from his starting point. Then, at thirty-four to thirty-eight feet from the back edge of the box, there will be another checkpoint. This checkpoint is used by the coach or a spotter. The athlete does *not* look at this mark since it is so close to the take-off. The "thirty-six foot" mark is four strides from the

62

take-off. The rationale for having this checkpoint in addition to the checkpoint at the take-off spot is that the vaulter can make adjustments in the last four strides that will make it appear as though he did take off properly. Thus, if the vaulter is "on" at "thirty-six feet," he will be "on" at the take-off (see Figure 7.1 for a typical run and checkpoint pattern).

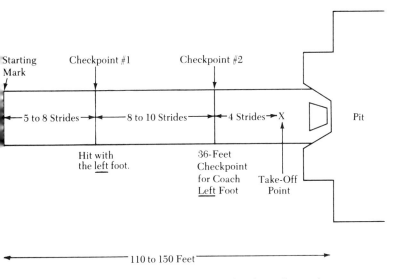

FIGURE 7.1. *Stride Pattern for the Pole Vault*

Note that the left foot is used as the checkpoint foot. A right-handed vaulter's first stride is with the left foot; the "eighty-six foot" check mark is hit with the left foot; the "thirty-six foot" mark is hit with the left foot; and the take-off is with the left foot. If the vaulter is left-handed, all the checkpoints are hit with the *right* foot. Why should each mark be hit with the same foot? The reason is simple; it gives an element of consistency to the athlete's performance.

Pole Grip and Carry

Because grips are becoming higher and higher, there is less adherence to the old principle of keeping the tip of the pole below nose level. Generally speaking, the pole is carried at a slight diagonal across the body. It is to the vaulter's advantage to keep the tip of the pole as low as possible, preferably at nose level. As the vaulter approaches the box, he drops the tip of the pole and brings it around to a position where he can drive the pole straight into the box. This sequence begins at about thirty-six feet, or four strides, from the box; the shift for planting about two strides from the box.

The Plant

If one assumes the run to be correct, the first really critical point of the vault is *the plant*. Nearly all problems or faults that occur during the vault can be traced to a mistake during the plant. If one assumes that the pole has been put in a line with the box during the approach, the vaulter can concentrate on driving straight into the box. This is accomplished by driving the pole forward with the right arm. The right arm is driven upward-forward from a position just behind the hip to a position just above and in front of the forehead. Some vaulters may bring the hand through in an underhand shift; some may bring the hand more overhead; the majority will be "straight through." Regardless of the style of shifting used, *the right hand must end up in front of and above the forehead* (see Figure 7.2).

FIGURE 7.2. *Pole Position at the Plant*

The left hand takes an active part in the planting sequence in acting as a guide to direct the pole into the box. Once the pole is firmly planted against the back of the box, the left hand and arm also are pressed vigorously into the pole. This requires not only great strength in the muscles of the arm but also in the muscles of the shoulder girdle.

The overall feeling during the plant phase should be one of extending the body and driving into the pole. The vaulter should feel as though he is behind and under the pole. The right leg is then driven upward as if the vaulter were taking another step. At this point, the right knee is maintained in a flexed position. As the toes of the left foot leave the ground, the left leg should be *fully* extended in driving the body off the ground. It is very important that the left leg be fully extended at the completion of the plant (see Figure 7.3 for an illustration of the planting sequence).

The Swing

As soon as the vaulter's left foot leaves the ground, the *swing* phase begins. During this phase, the left arm bends more as the vaulter progresses through the swing. At the same time, it is acting to keep the center of gravity from swinging past the pole. The elbow of the right arm is kept in a position near the plane that bisects the body. With the elbow in this position, the shoulder is in an externally rotated position and can be locked so that it is prevented from hyperextending to the point where the vaulter would lose control of his body. If this position is not maintained, the effect is the same as a weak left arm; the body will not only move forward too fast but will rotate slightly.

During the early stages of the swing, the body is moving relatively slowly as the pole bends. As the center of gravity starts accelerating upward, the action of the legs becomes evident. There are basically three styles of leg action all of which have the purpose of placing the vaulter in an inverted position.

Two-leg swing. After the initial lead by the right leg, the left leg "catches-up" to the right as the vaulter starts to upset. At the point at which the legs are in a parallel position, the knees are slightly bent.

Left-Leg Lead. As the vaulter drives off the ground, the right leg leads as usual, but as the left leg loses contact, it begins a very rapid

Do not allow this elbow
to pass the pole.

Get full extension of take-off leg;
drive forward and upward.

FIGURE 7.3. *Extension at the Take-off*

pendular action which results in its catching up with and going beyond the right leg. This is a very dramatic, explosive type of maneuver and has the effect of putting the vaulter in an inverted position relatively quickly. As long as pressure is maintained by the
arms, this style also puts a great deal of "energy" into the pole in a
short period of time. At the top of the vault, the athlete will have a de-
layed finish but, again, it will be very explosive.

Right-Leg Lead. This style approaches what was once standard
vaulting technique. The right leg again leads from the take-off and
continues to lead throughout the vault. The left leg begins to move

in a pendular manner and approaches the right but never quite catches up to it. The right leg maintains a flexed knee position of about 120 degrees. This style facilitates a smooth transition from the inverted position to the finish. (Figure 7.4 illustrates each of these techniques).

No matter which of these techniques the young athlete eventually settles on, the important point is that he must rotate his body into an inverted vertical position. The purpose of each of these techniques is to aid the vaulter in maintaining the inverted position. When learning the event, it is best for the athlete to start with the right-leg lead.

The Finish

The finish starts as the pole begins to straighten. At this point, the feet are extending skyward and the head is the body part which is closest to the ground. The vaulter pulls vigorously with the right arm, and as he pulls, the body rotates while moving upward. Once the center of gravity of the vaulter elevates past the hand hold, a push is initiated, first with the left arm, then with the right arm. The head is maintained in a "down" position, and the thumbs of both hands are rotated inward as the vaulter comes off the pole.

Learning the Event

There are many approaches to learning the techniques of pole vaulting. The one included in the following section is just one of the many. In this description, it is assumed that the vaulter is right-handed.

The Grip and Carry

Standing at attention with the pole held upright on the right side of the body and the tip resting on the ground, the vaulter places the left hand on the pole by reaching across the chest at armpit level. He then reaches up along the pole with the right hand and grips it at as high a position as possible while maintaining a flat-footed position.

He next brings the pole to a carrying position with the tip somewhere around head level. The right elbow should be flexed about 90 degrees and straight back. The pole will pass from front to rear near the crest of the ileum (hip bone).

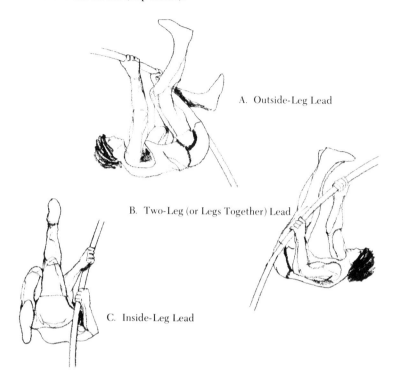

A. Outside-Leg Lead

B. Two-Leg (or Legs Together) Lead

C. Inside-Leg Lead

FIGURE 7.4. *Pole Vault Techniques*

Planting and Swinging on the Pole

At this point, the vaulter stands with the tip of the pole touching the ground outside of and adjacent to the left foot. He rocks back on the right foot; he then steps forward and swings on the pole as though trying to vault over a small creek. As control is gained, he places the pole farther out in front of the body and swings by taking a longer step (see Figure 7.6). Throughout these exercises, the hand grip remains the same. As confidence is gained, the vaulter should raise the grip six to twelve inches, take one or two steps, and repeat the support and swing. The objective at this point is to try and see how *far* he can vault.

FIGURE 7.5. *Learning to Grip the Pole*

At this point, it is time to start thinking about knee action and "rocking back." The vaulter simply pulls the knees up *a little* as he swings from the ground. He should not forget to bring the feet back down to the ground after lifting the knees! He practices this until he can rock back with the knees at head level and then land on the feet.

He then raises the grip another eight to twelve inches and goes to the vaulting box where he practices shifting the pole from the carrying position to the plant. At this time, he does not swing up; instead, he simply plants the pole by driving the pole forward and "punching'' the back of the box. In the finished plant position, the right hand is directly over the head, while the left hand is about fifteen inches below the right hand, and the pole is in a plane which bisects the body. The planted foot (left) is directly beneath the pole.

After achieving a feeling for the shift and plant, the vaulter starts taking short running approaches (five to nine steps), planting, and swinging into the pit. Again, it is important to see how *far* into the pit the vaulter can go. This requires ''riding'' the pole. After this exercise, the vaulter starts pulling the knees upward, rocking, and landing in the pit on his upper back (see Figure 7.6). From here, the grip can be raised and the run lengthened. After learning to upset, the vaulter can initiate his work on the finish by a pulling action with the arms. As the pull is started, the body rotates in spiral fashion around the pole. In a continuing motion, the arms then extend as the vaulter releases from the pole. The final step is to vault over a bar! Although this event may seem complex, it is important to remember one point: All seventeen-foot vaulters were once six-foot vaulters.

Basic Rules for the Pole Vault

1. The vaulting pole may be of bamboo, metal, or fiber glass and be of unlimited size and weight. It shall have no assisting devices other than two layers of adhesive tape applied with uniform thickness.

2. The pit shall have a minimum width and depth of sixteen feet by twelve feet.

3. The runway shall have a minimum length of 125 feet.

4. A legal jump is one in which the vaulter passes over the bar without displacing it.

5. A missed vault occurs when:
   a. The bar is displaced by the vaulter or pole.
   b. The vaulter leaves the ground in an attempted vault and fails to clear the bar.
   c. Any part of the vaulter's body or pole touches the ground beyond the plane of the stopboard.
   d. During the vault, the vaulter displaces his upper hand higher on the pole or moves his lower hand above his upper hand.

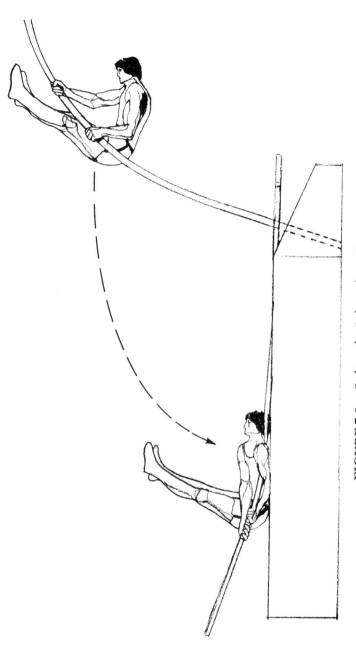

FIGURE 7.6. *Riding the Pole and Landing in the Pit*

The Throwing Events

8

The Shot Put

Shot "putting" appears to be a strange name. Why not shot "throwing" instead? Upon examination of the rules, one sees that the shot put event is described in a fashion that eliminates throwing the shot. If one actually tried to throw the shot as a sixteen-pound baseball, he would very seriously injure his arm and shoulder. In reality, the shot is "put" from a position from above shoulder level.

Since 1952, exceptional improvement has been made in the shot put with the introduction of Parry O'Brian's technique of starting with the body rotated 180 degrees from the direction of putting. Previously, the shoulders were rotated only 90 degrees from the direction of throwing. The record has improved from about fifty-seven feet to well over seventy feet in a span of about fifteen years.

Essentially, the event consists of moving across a ring or circle of seven feet diameter and putting the shot as far as possible. The shot must land in a sector of approximately forty-five degrees from the center of the putting surface. The shot for junior high school athletes weighs eight pounds; for high school, twelve pounds; and for college, sixteen pounds.

Elements of the Event

Holding the Shot

The shot should rest at the base of the fingers (at the top part of the palm). The fingers should be wrapped around the iron ball. The ball is placed a little closer to the thumb and index finger because the major portion of the strength of the hand is in this part. If at first the athlete is too weak to hold the shot in this position, he should rest it in the palm of his hand. Then as he grows stronger, he can place the ball higher towards the fingers. Champion shot

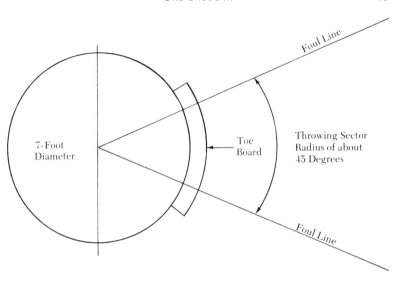

FIGURE 8.1. *The Throwing Sector*

putters release the ball from their fingers, putting additional snap and momentum into the put.

The shot is rested against the neck just below the jaw bone midway between the chin and angle of the jaw bone. In this position, the elbow of the throwing arm is down. One could imagine the ball being held or sitting on top of a rod (the arm).

FIGURE 8.2. *Holding the Shot*

FIGURE 8.3. *Position of the Shot Relative to the Body*

Putting the Shot

There are four phases to the shot put—the start, drive, lift and turn, and release and reverse.

The Start. As with any other venture, getting started is the key to success. The putter faces 180 degrees from the direction he is throwing. His driving leg (the right leg for right-handed putters) is placed near the back edge of the circle and his other leg slightly toward the center of the ring. His thoughts should concentrate on "bend," "sink," "drive." "Bend" at the waist; "sink" at the knee; then start the next phase—"drive" across the ring. The drive is often referred to as the glide.

At first, the bend and sink will feel uncomfortable and disjointed, especially when the athlete is trying to coordinate the lead leg. The athlete should always start from an upright position in which the shoulders are as relaxed as possible, with the head *slightly* forward and down.

The lead leg works in rhythm with the "bend," "sink," "drive" sequence. At "bend," the left leg is extended backward and upward for balance. At the command "sink," it is brought down to a position adjacent to the right leg and then during the "drive" is forcibly extended toward the toe board—touching the toe board at "eleven o'clock."

The Drive. After sinking, the right leg is explosively extended causing the putter to move across the ring; the right foot is replanted in the center of the ring on a straight line with the back of the ring and the middle of the stop board. The right foot should be at an angle of 45 degrees. The purpose of the drive phase is to initiate a fast movement by the athlete prior to the lift and turn.

The Lift and Turn. As the drive is completed, the actual put starts with the lift and turn. From the center of the ring, the athlete's body is over his right leg with the shoulders still essentially 180 degrees from the direction of putting. With the lead leg near or touching the toe board, there is another explosive drive from the right leg; only this time the trunk and upper body begin turning and lifting toward the front of the ring. The left elbow is brought forcibly upward-outward and around, causing the putter to open and face toward the direction of putting.

Force is generated from the driving leg straight through the right hip into the right torso on into the right shoulder and finally into the metal ball. The arm acts as a link for transfer of the generated force from the shoulder to the hand holding the "iron."

The Release and Reverse. As the body begins to open up and the arm is uncoiling, the right elbow is raised from a position close to the body to an almost horizontal position. As the arm nears complete extension, the ball leaves the hand. The shot is snapped off the top of the palm and fingers with a final, complete, arm extension. Sometimes, the force in this phase of the put is so great in conjunction with the lift and turn that both feet leave the ground.

In order to keep from going out of the ring and fouling, the athlete must check his forward momentum, doing what is called a "reverse." This simply means that the left foot is lifted from the ring surface and rapidly replaced by the right foot. The putter thus ends up by balancing on his right foot.

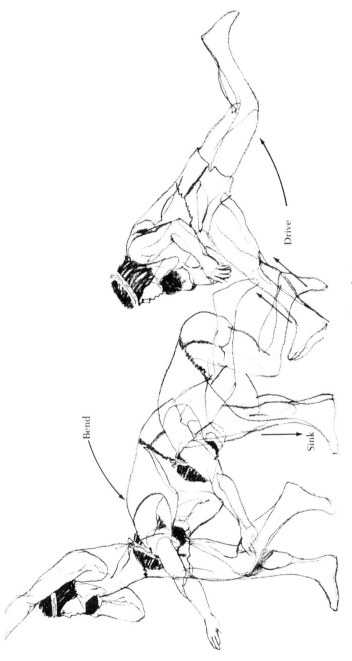

FIGURE 8.4. *Bend, Sink, Drive*

Drive

Bend

Sink

78

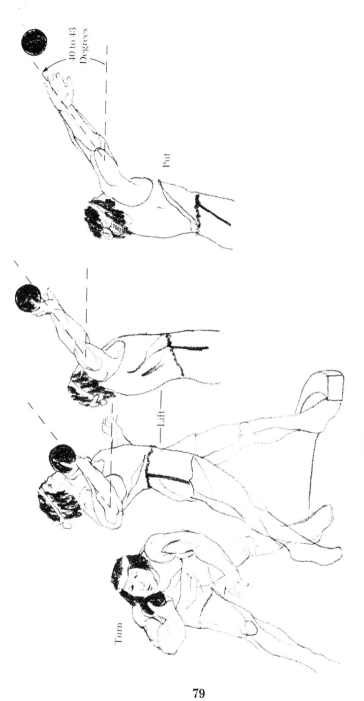

40 to 43
Degrees

Put

Lift

Turn

FIGURE 8.5. *The Turn, Lift, and Put*

79

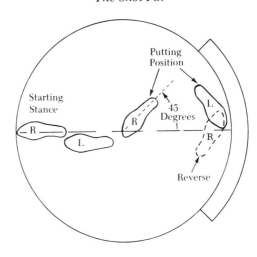

FIGURE 8.6. *Foot Pattern in Putting the Shot*

Learning the Event

The best way to learn the event is to start with the ending! The putter simply holds the metal ball in his hand in the correct position, bends at the knees slightly, then uncoils with the knees and "pushes" the shot high into the air. Weight is evenly distributed on both feet and the shot is released straightaway. There is no trunk twisting involved.

After this has been accomplished, the next step is to spread the legs slightly, turning the right foot 45 degrees. This position allows the putter to transfer his body weight over the right foot. By putting his weight over the right foot, he is almost forced to twist his trunk so that his chest is now on a line straight above the right knee. From this position, the "lift" and "finish" can be practiced. As he explosively straightens the right leg, the trunk rotates and lifts. It is simply a matter of extending the putting arm to release the ball.

The problem now is reduced to achieving the start ("bend," "sink," and "drive") to the center of the ring. At first, it is best to do this without the shot. Then, of course, the start should be practiced with the heavy shot cradled in the palm of the hand. The athlete should now stop at the center of the ring and check his position: right foot in middle of ring turned 45 degrees, weight over the right leg, shoulders rotated 180 degrees from the putting direction (i.e., pointing toward "six o'clock").

The ideal angle of release is about 40 to 43 degrees. With this angle, the trajectory is achieved which will cause the ball to land the furthest from the putter.

Basic Rules for the Shot Put

1. The shot shall be a "perfect" shape without indentation which might act as a grip.

2. The shot shall have the following specifications:

   a. *Collegiate:* Weight not less than sixteen pounds (7.257 kilograms), a minimum diameter of 4.331 inches (110 millimeters), and maximum diameter of 5.118 inches (5.44 kilograms).

   b. *High School:* Weight not less than twelve pounds (5.44 kilograms).

3. The putting circle shall have a diameter of seven feet.

4. The stopboard shall be an arc of wood anchored with its inner edge coinciding with the inner edge of the circle. It shall be four feet long (inside edge), four inches high, and 4.5 inches wide.

5. The competitors shall put the shot in such a way that it lands in a sector of approximately 45 degrees radiating from the center of the circle.

6. A legal put shall be made from within the circle and have the shot land in the sector. The put must be made from the shoulder with one hand and not be allowed to drop below the shoulder. (Distance is measured to the lesser one-quarter inch.)

7. A foul put is said to occur when the competitor:

   a. Causes the shot to fall on or outside the lines marking the sector.

b. Touches any part of his body or clothing, before the put is marked, to:
   1. Any surface of the metal band except the inside surface.
   2. Any part of the painted line.
   3. Any surface of the stopboard except its inside surface.
   4. Any area outside the circle.
c. Puts a shot not conforming to the legal standards.
d. Leaves the circle from the front half of the circle.
e. Wears any illegal device or tapes on his putting arm, wrists, hand, or fingers.

9

The Discus

Of all of the symbols of sports and athletics, the most widely known is that of the Discus Thrower, or Discobolus, by Myron of ancient Greece. The discus throw was an event in the ancient Greek Olympics and with only minor modifications is included in today's Olympic competition. Not only is the discus throw included in the modern Olympic Games, it is included among all levels of competition as an integral part of the program.

The discus is thrown from a circle of eight feet, two and one-half inches in diameter into a sector of approximately 65 degrees. The thrower starts at the back of the ring facing 180 degrees from the direction of throwing and progresses across the ring. While moving across the ring, the discus thrower makes one and a half turns.

There is an additional element to the discus throw that is not present in the shot put event. The shape of the disc makes it an aerodynamic foil, similar to an airplane wing. As a result, when the disc is thrown, the athlete tries to make the disc spin and to throw it *into* the wind. If this is done properly, the disc will "lift" or "float" in the air and sail a few feet farther.

Elements of the Event

Gripping and Releasing the Disc

The best way to get the feeling of holding the disc properly is to hold it at the side as if it were a book. The first joint of each finger should curl over the edge of the disc (see Figure 9.1). The fingers are spread evenly, with the thumb flat against the surface of the disc.

To get the proper feeling of releasing the disc, the athlete tries to roll the disc forward along the ground. The disc should come off the hand on the thumb side (as opposed to the little finger). The middle finger and first finger should be the last to touch the disc as it leaves the hand. After learning to roll the disc along the ground, the next step is to throw the disc easily in the air in the same fashion as rolling it along the ground (i.e., it is thrown straight away from the athlete describing a peaked trajectory and is made to land on edge). Eventually, the disc is thrown a little harder and snapped off the first two fingers. It is important to remember to throw *easily* at first and then gradually take a more vigorous step and throw.

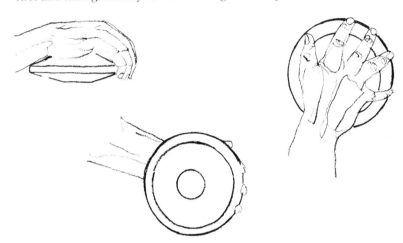

FIGURE 9.1. *Gripping the Disc*

Throwing the Discus

As with the shot put, there are four distinct phases of the event— the preliminary swing, the turn, the throw, and, finally, the reverse. The ring may be divided into front and back half with the points of the clock as references.

Preliminary Swings. Assuming a position at the back of the circle with the feet at approximately "five o'clock" and "seven o'clock," the athlete makes two or three relaxed twists. The back is facing the direction of throwing and the knees are slightly bent. The swings involve rotating the trunk and arms, shifting weight from foot to foot, to establish a pattern of rhythm and motion. As this is done, the athlete should imagine that he is sitting on an old fashioned piano stool that swivels. As he twists to the right he draws the left arm toward the chest as the right arm is extended and behind him. In returning the rotation, the left arm remains bent as the right arm comes around.

The Turn.   This phase of the event involves one and one-half revolutions with very distinct footwork. Once the turn is started, the thrower should concentrate on driving toward the front of the ring with a continuous acceleration. In other words, the slowest part of the motion should be at the back of the ring while the fastest part is at the front.

The footwork involves pivoting on the left foot, landing on the right foot in the center of the ring, and then planting the left foot at about "eleven o'clock." While pivoting on the left foot (see Figure 9.2), the athlete drives his left shoulder and head downward and forward. (He can get the feel of this move by imagining peeking over his left shoulder.) The right foot also is driven around but is kept low. One tries to lead with the right knee (see Figure 9.3). After the right foot has been planted in the center of the ring, the foot pivots approximately 180 degrees as the left foot is being planted at about "eleven o'clock." Planting the left foot at "eleven o'clock" puts the thrower in a position to put his hips into the throw.

The position of both arms is important throughout the turn. The left arm in a sense leads the throw. Most throwers, upon starting the turn, will tend to straighten the left arm while swinging it around; then, after getting to the center of the ring, they will bend the arm and, on the final phase of the turn, straighten it with the idea of putting a final additional thrust of force when delivering the disc.

The hand of the throwing arm is kept as far away from the body and as far in back of the body as is possible. The palm of the hand is downward. At this point, most beginners will have difficulty holding the disc; however, if the arm is in continuous motion, centrifugal force will keep the disc pressed against the fingertips.

The Throw.   Once the left foot has been planted at the front of the ring, the thrower is ready to release the disc. The right arm now is pulled through by the large muscles of the chest and shoulder. The right hip is snapped toward the front of the ring as a result of the right leg drive. An additional "snap" is imparted to the disc as it

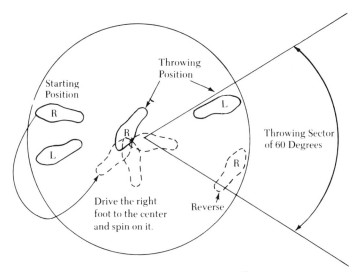

FIGURE 9.2. *Footwork*

FIGURE 9.3. *Discus Throwing Techniques*

comes off the first and middle fingers. This "snap" will help in increasing the spin on the disc, thus taking greater advantage of its aerodynamic qualities.

The optimum angle of release is partially dependent upon three things: the velocity, direction, and steadiness of the wind; the angle of inclination of the disc as related to the wind; and the precise manner in which the thrower applies force to the disc (i.e., his technique). Basically, however, it is safe to say that an angle of 30 degrees with the horizontal is the best.

After releasing the disc, the right arm should follow through beyond the ring, then diagonally down and across to the left side of the body.

The Reverse. This phase is just the natural consequence of a well-executed throw. The right foot will come down at the front of the ring with the left foot leaving the ground. Sometimes the thrower will spin around on the right foot as a result of his natural momentum.

Learning the Event

After learning to hold the disc as described above, one of the most useful practices is to "scale" the disc from the front of the throwing circle. The athlete takes a stance that approximates his position when the right foot is in the center of the ring and the left foot is at the front of the ring at about "eleven o'clock." The right foot may be forward of the center of the ring when "scaling."

While scaling, the athlete can concentrate on several very important components of the event: right leg extension with forward drive of the right hip; position of right arm and left arm; angle of release; and the "snap" and follow-through.

The next important element to learn is the turn. This may be practiced without the disc until it is well "grooved." The athlete starts the swing, pivots to the center of the ring, stops, checks his position, then follows through with the rest of the motion.

Follow-up practice of the swing and turn should be accomplished by using the disc and going through the complete motion. At the point of release, the athlete simply relaxes and allows the disc to float into the sector only a short distance (twenty to fifty feet away).

Basic Rules for the Discus

1. The discus shall be composed of a smooth metal rim, permanently attached to a wood or plastic body, with metal plates set flush into the sides of the body and located in the exact center of the discus.

2. The discus shall meet the following general specifications:

    a. *Collegiate:*   Weigh not less than four pounds 6.548 ounces (two kilograms) and have an outer diameter of between 8.622 inches (219 millimeters) and 8.7 inches (221 millimeters).

    b. *High School:*   Weigh not less than three pounds nine ounces (1.616 kilograms) and have an outer diameter of 8.25 inches.

3. The circle shall have a diameter of eight feet 2.5 inches.

4. The throwing sector shall be formed by two lines radiating from the center of the circle at an angle of 60 degrees.

5. The measurement of a throw shall be from the nearest edge of the first mark made by the discus to the inside edge of the circle (to the lesser one-half inch).

6. A foul throw shall be said to occur if, after entering the circle and starting his throw, the competitor:

    a. Causes the discus to fall on or outside the lines marking the sector.

    b. Touches, before the line is marked, with any part of the body or clothing:

        1. Any surface of the metal band except the inside surface.
        2. Any part of the painted line.
        3. The area outside the circle.

    c. Leaves the circle from the front half.

    d. Throws an implement which does not conform to the legal requirements.

10

The Javelin

The javelin throw had been one of the events of the ancient Greek games and was introduced in the modern Olympics in 1908. Due to the danger of injury to spectators and other athletes, the javelin event has not been accepted as widely in the United States as most other events of track and field. The event has been popular primarily on the East and West Coasts but is now gaining in the Midwest. It is truly an event that blends the speed and strength of the athlete into the long, graceful trajectory of the implement.

The basic rule of the event dictates that the javelin shall not weigh less than 800 grams (1.76 lbs.) and should have an overall length of between 260 and 270 centimeters (eight feet six inches to eight feet 10.25 inches). The throwing area is very precisely defined. The run-up or approach is not to exceed 120 feet, with the approach lane being thirteen feet wide and the foul line an arc described with a radius of twenty-six feet three inches. The throwing sector lines are drawn using the center of the twenty-fix feet three inch circle as a guide and intersecting the juncture of the foul line and alley line (see Figure 10.1).

Description of the Javelin

In Figure 10.2, the various parts of the javelin are illustrated. The tip or point is the part that breaks ground when the javelin lands. The grip or cord is the area where the thrower holds the javelin, while the tail is the part of the implement farthest from the tip. The tail of the javelin should never be used to break the ground, as it can be bent easily. Once the balance of the javelin is destroyed, it looses the delicately tooled aerodynamic qualities and will vibrate while in flight. The shaft is made of wood, aluminum, or some other lightweight metal, while the tip is made of steel or some other harder metal.

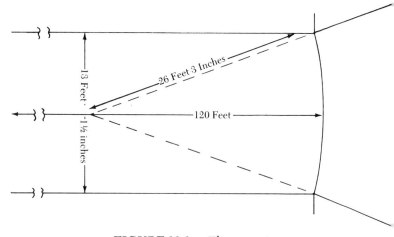

FIGURE 10.1.   *Throwing Area*

Elements of the Event

Gripping the Javelin

There are two accepted means of gripping the javelin. The first involves locking the middle finger on the cord of the javelin, while the second involves locking the first finger on the cord. The first method is preferred by most throwers because it allows the thrower to place the first finger higher on the shaft for control of the tail of the javelin. With both grips, the javelin lies diagonally across the palm of the hand.

Throwing the Javelin

As with the other throwing events, the javelin throw has four basic parts which have to be smoothly integrated from start to finish. The four phases are: the run or approach; preparation for throwing; the throw; and the follow-through.

The Approach.   As he would other field events requiring an approach (pole vault, long jump, high jump, triple jump), the athlete

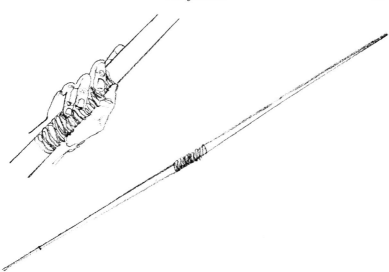

FIGURE 10.2. *Gripping the Javelin*

should have checkpoints along the route. These are incorporated to develop a consistent approach to the throwing area. Younger javelin throwers will take seven or nine steps to the checkpoint, while more experienced throwers who have learned to control their momentum may take eleven or thirteen steps to this point. The reason for utilizing an odd number of steps is that it is a sound idea to hit the checkpoint on the same foot that the thrower starts on (usually the left foot). From the checkpoint, the athlete enters the throwing phase and the footwork becomes a part of the throw.

There are two ways of carrying the javelin to the checkpoint during the approach. The first is to carry it satchel style with the tail pointed toward the throwing area. As the checkpoint is approached, the thrower swings the javelin forward and upward to a position over the shoulder in preparation for straightening the arm. The second method is to start with the javelin held over the shoulder with the tip pointed toward the throwing area. The first method allows for greater approach speed but requires a well-coordinated move in shifting the javelin over the shoulder. The second method does not allow as rapid a buildup of speed as the first but eliminates swinging the javelin up from the side.

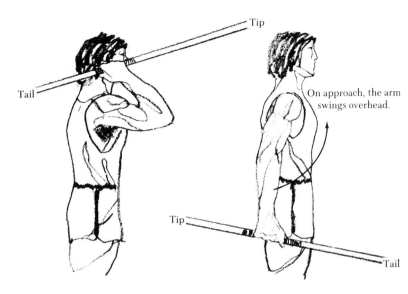

FIGURE 10.3.   *Carrying the Javelin*

Preparation for Throwing   As the left foot hits the checkpoint, the javelin is pulled back along the body, the throwing arm is locked, and the shaft extends upward along the arm and past the cheek bone. Counting the contact of the left foot with the ground as the first step, the athlete draws the javelin back over the next four strides. As he draws the javelin back, he rotates the body slightly and forces a cross-over of the fourth step.

The Throw.   After the crossover, between steps three and four, the left foot is "blocked" (heel hits first), thereby halting the forward movement of the athlete. At this point, the javelin is forcefully pulled forward and upward along a straight line. At this point, there also should be a great deal of pressure on the left leg, as it is absorbing the forward momentum of the body. The elbow should come through high and lead the throwing hand. The head will be slightly to the left so that the spear may be brought through straight. The javelin must be "whipped" out at an angle close to 40 degrees.

FIGURE 10.4. *Preparation for Throwing*

93

FIGURE 10.5. *The Throw*

The Follow-Through. To keep from being carried over the foul line, the thrower must bring his right leg through rapidly and balance on it to regain control over his body. When leaving the throwing area, the athlete must walk out of the area behind the extensions of the foul line (see Figure 10.6).

Learning the Event

Remembering that the javelin must be released straight without any side arm or round house throwing motion, it is best to first start

FIGURE 10.6. *The Follow-through*

95

throwing the javelin at targets on the ground ten to fifteen feet away. Starting with the javelin in the overhead position, the athlete takes aim at the target and then draws the javelin straight back over the shoulder, rotating the arm inward to keep the javelin along the cheek bone. The palm of the hand should be skyward. This latter position also facilitates leading with the elbow while throwing.

From this position, the athlete steps directly toward the target and snaps the javelin through overhead. If thrown properly, the javelin should stick in the ground with the tail pointed straight back towards the thrower. When withdrawing the javelin from the ground, it is important to pull it out along the same path it entered, as though withdrawing an arrow from a target or a dart from a dart board. The javelin should never be pried from the ground.

As control is gained in hitting the target with the javelin straight, the distance gradually should be increased to about fifty or sixty feet.

At this point, the athlete may start working on the cross step and throw by starting from about twenty feet again and working up to fifty or sixty feet. The pattern is to draw the javelin back, cross step with the right foot, block with the left foot, and throw or "draw," "cross," "block," "throw."

After achieving control with the cross step, the athlete proceeds to take a short, easy approach (five to seven steps), cross, block, and throw to target. From this point onward, he may start working on refining his style and technique and throwing for distance. As the distance thrown increases, the trajectory or path of the javelin takes a more arching form until the "ideal" release angle of 40 degrees with the horizontal is achieved.

Special Practice Tips

In addition to the basic conditioning that all athletes should receive, the javelin thrower has several special techniques to practice.

The Cross Step. The cross step is a very critical component of the javelin throw and as such deserves special attention. Because it is essential to maintain as much as possible the momentum built up by the approach, the javelin thrower must be as able to execute the cross step as he would any other running stride. In the words of John

Powell, ''The rear leg is brought across the front leg in a fast, snappy action, heel to shin. Both feet are momentarily off the ground as this is done. The rear foot lands on outer border directly across the line of direction of throw.'' [1]

The cross step may be practiced by running ''sprints'' while crossing. The athlete runs on a line so that direction can be learned and become almost instinctive. At first, he repeats short distances of about twenty yards several times (five before throwing practice and five after). Gradually, he increases the distance to fifty yards or more. Some of the best javelin throwers in the world will go 100 yards.

The Throw. To simulate the throwing action and build strength at the same time, an elastic line anchored to a post or ring in the ground may be utilized. The resistance may be increased or decreased by lengthening or shortening the elastic line. A modification of this technique would be to use a rope, then work isometrically [2] in various positions by changing the length of the rope.

Basic Rules for the Javelin

1. The javelin shall consist of three parts: a metal head, a shaft, and a cord grip. The shaft may be constructed of either wood or metal to which a metal head terminating in a sharp point is attached.

2. The javelin shall have a minimum weight of 800 grams and an overall length of between eight feet 6.375 inches (260 centimeters) and eight feet 10.25 inches (270 centimeters). (*Note:* More details concerning dimensions appear in the rule book.)

3. The cord grip shall be about the center of gravity without thongs, notches, or indentations.

4. The foul line shall be made in the shape of an arc with a radius of twenty-six feet three inches (eight meters). The distance

---

[1]John Powell, *Track and Field Fundamentals for Teacher and Coach* (Champaign, Illinois: Stipes Publishing Co., 1962), p. 62

[2]Each position is held for six seconds, followed by thirty seconds of rest, and repeated three times.

FIGURE 10.7. *Javelin Training Device*

between its extremities shall be thirteen feet 1.5 inches (four meters) measured straight across.

5. The measurement shall be made from the nearest edge of the first mark made by the javelin to the inside circumference of the arc, with such mark measured along a line from the mark to the center of the circle of which the arc is a part (e.g., the measuring tape must be extended through the center of the circle twenty-six feet three inches from the foul line).

6. The javelin must be held by the grip and the throw made from behind the arc (foul line). It must fall within the sector and the point must strike the ground before any part of the shaft.

7. The thrower cannot allow his body to rotate through 360 degrees at any time during the approach or delivery.

8. The delivery must be made with a distinct above-the-shoulders of the throwing arm.

9. A foul shall be said to occur when the competitor:

   a. Causes the javelin to land on or outside the lines marking the sector.

   b. Throws the javelin so that the tip of the metal head does not strike the ground before any other part of the javelin.

   c. Touches with any part of his body or apparel:

      1. Any surface of the stopboard (foul line).

      2. The run-up lines.

      3. The area outside the stopboard or run-up lines.

   d. Fails to hold the javelin by the grip.

11

Conditioning And Training

In track and field, the process of preparing for competition involves aspects of both conditioning and training. Conditioning is the process by which one works to improve the foundations of physical fitness, including muscular strength, muscular (or local) endurance, cardio-respiratory (or general) endurance, and flexibility. These components of physical fitness, possessed at an optimal level, will enable the athlete to perform at high levels of proficiency. Conditioning is generally thought of as taking place either in the off-season or during periods of low-level competition.

Training involves structured practice of skills in a particular event. While training, the athlete will invariably repeat a particular movement over and over thus achieving improvement in his *condition*. A triple jumper will hop fifty yards on one leg, simulating the hop phase of the event. Not only is he refining the rhythm and form of the hop but he is also improving the strength and endurance in the "hopping" leg by *overload*. The distance runner surely spends the majority of his time seeking to improve cardio-respiratory fitness, while spending very little time concentrating on running style. The pole vaulter does bent-arm pull-overs as an exercise specifically designed to strengthen the musculature of the upper arm and shoulder girdle. The exercise can be done both in the off-season and in-season. With improved strength of the shoulders and arms, he will have greater stability during the plant and early phases of the pole-bend. A hurdler will do specific flexibility exercises for the trunk and hips in order to improve his efficiency over the hurdles. Thus, the concepts of conditioning and training will fuse into one depending upon the time, circumstances, and objectives.

Overload and Progressive Resistance Exercise

Overload, one fundamental concept of improving physical fitness, was mentioned in the preceding paragraph. Initially, the overload principle was applied to programs which had the objective of improving strength. Basically, overload refers to applying a sufficiently large resistance (weights or isometric devices) to a group of muscles in order to stimulate an increase in strength. But what is "a sufficiently large resistance" that will elicit such an increase?

Strength Programs

With an isometric program, where the resistance is so great that the muscle group will not shorten noticeably (in other words, where there is no joint movement), it has been stated that an effort of 60 percent of maximum isometric strength held for six seconds is sufficient to elicit a strength gain. Thus, if one has available a device (cable tensiometer) for measuring isometric strength and finds that he has a biceps strength reading of 100 pounds with the arm bent at 90 degrees, pulling with sixty pounds of tension during training is sufficient to provide a stimulus. The exercise should be repeated three times for each muscle group. (For further information on this topic, the reader is referred to Olson.[1])

Utilizing an isotonic program (weight training), overload is defined in the Progressive Resistance Exercise (or PRE) system of training. DeLorme developed the concepts of PRE during World War II in aiding wounded servicemen to recuperation. The procedure for establishing the overload resistance is to take a lifting bar and load it with a weight that can be lifted ten times. Finding the proper resistance may take two or three sessions in the weight room. Work with this established resistance continues until the weight can be lifted fifteen times. The last two or three lifts in a set should be near maximum effort. Once fifteen repetitions are achieved in a set, the bar is reloaded with five or ten pounds so that only ten repetitions can be completed again. Since this is a simplified explanation of PRE, the reader is again referred to Olsen for further explanation and detail.

Cardiovascular Program

Overload is also a valid concept for improving cardio-respiratory conditioning and speed. There are numerous training "methods" for running conditioning, but the key to how one trains lies in what competitive distances are being run. By analyzing the events, one could design his own program. Stated as simply as pos-

---

[1]Edward C. Olson, *Conditioning Fundamentals* (Columbus, Ohio: Charles E. Merrill Publishing Co., 1967).

sible: A sprinter must engage in sprint-type activities; a distance runner must engage in long training runs; a middle-distance runner must blend fast running with volume to achieve his goals. Although there are departures from this basic concept as certain running "fads" appear, most runners practice these approaches. There are some very sound physiological reasons for the validity of the above-stated concepts. An excellent, understandable explanation of the physiological basis of training and conditioning can be found in Mathews and Fox.[1]

The idea is now emerging from the literature on exercise physiology that it is perhaps not necessary or even advisable to train "hard" every day. Based upon knowledge acquired through muscle biopsy studies, is it now known that glycogen stores (energy source) will be reduced to very low levels after a very strenuous workout. Evidence indicates that it takes from forty-eight to seventy-two hours for glycogen levels to be restored to nominal values. Thus, a strenuous workout followed by one or two days of *very* easy training would seem to have merit. A practical illustration of this approach can be found in the coaching of Bill Bowerman at the University of Oregon. With certain departures, the "Bowerman Method" of "one hard day—two easy days" training is practiced at the University of Oregon.

SUMMARY

It has been the purpose of this chapter to introduce certain basic concepts of conditioning to the novice. Although specific training routines have been omitted, key references have been provided within this chapter and in the reference list at the conclusion of this text. Most of the references are readily available and can serve as a rich source of materials for the aspiring athlete and coach. Upon inspection, the reader will find that a number of training and conditioning hints have been built into each chapter.

---

[1]D.K. Mathews and E.L. Fox, *The Physiological Basis of Physical Education and Athletics* (Philadelphia: W.B. Saunders Company, 1971).

Appendix

Using the Performance Tables

The performance tables are based upon the compilation of results achieved by nonvarsity college freshmen in physical education classes and are to be used in college physical education classes. The scales range from zero to one hundred points with the *mean* performance in each event equaling fifty points. Thus, it takes an exceptional performance to score one hundred points.

Odd events, such as the standing triple jump, 120-yard low hurdles, 60-yard dash (outdoors), and 50-foot approach triple jump, are included as a result of the author's attempts to find events in which the inexperienced college Freshman may compete with some safety and success.

The tables may be used for the following purposes:
1. To evaluate performance and progress in each event.
2. To compare performance in different events.
3. To provide a means of compiling team scores.
4. To provide a scoring table so that individuals may compare performances on several events.
5. To classify students into homogeneous groups.

As an example of the use of the Performance Tables Sid Sink and Andy Jugan competed in several events with the following results:

TABLE 1

	Andy		Sid	
Events	*Performance*	*Points*	*Performance*	*Points*
60 Yd. Dash	5´0˝	54	4´10˝	50
Standing Triple Jump	23´0˝	57	20´3˝	36
One-Mile Run	4:58	80	5:50	50
Shot Put	23´6˝	31	43´8˝	84
High Jump	4´2˝	34	5´1˝	56
Totals		206		246

Based upon the compilation of points in the five events, Sid performed better than Andy by a score of 246 to 206 points. Furthermore, they both performed above average in that an average score in each event would have given the two performers 200 points.

TABLE 2

Scale Score	100-Yd. Dash (Secs.)	220-Yd. Dash	60-Yd. Dash (Secs.)	440-Yd. Dash (Secs.)	880-Yd. Run (Min.:Secs.)	Standing Triple Jump (Ft.-In.)
1		31.8	8.6	83.3	2:58.5	15´ 7´´
2	14.3	31.7		82.9	2:58.0	15´ 8´´
3		31.6		82.5	2:57.5	15´ 10´´
4	14.2	31.5		82.1	2:57.0	16´ 0´´
5		31.4	8.5	81.7	2:56.5	16´ 1´´
6	14.1	31.3		81.3	2:56.0	16´ 3´´
7		31.2		80.9	2:55.5	16´ 4´´
8	14.0	31.1		80.5	2:55.0	16´ 6´´
9		31.0		80.1	2:54.5	16´ 8´´
10		30.9	8.4	79.7	2:54.0	16´ 9´´
11	13.9	30.8		79.3	2:53.5	16´ 11´´
12		30.7		78.9	2:53.0	17´ 0´´
13	13.8	30.6		78.5	2:52.5	17´ 2´´
14		30.5		78.1	2:52.0	17´ 4´´
15	13.7	30.4	8.3	77.7	2:51.5	17´ 5´´
16		30.3		77.3	2:51.0	17´ 7´´
17	13.6	30.2		76.9	2:50.5	17´ 8´´
18		30.1		76.5	2:50.0	17´ 10´´
19		30.0		76.1	2:49.5	18´ 0´´
20	13.5	29.9	8.2	75.7	2:49.0	18´ 1´´
21		29.8		75.3	2:48.5	18´ 3´´
22	13.4	29.7		74.9	2:48.0	18´ 4´´
23		29.6		74.5	2:47.5	18´ 6´´
24	13.3	29.5		74.1	2:47.0	18´ 8´´
25		29.4	8.1	73.7	2:46.5	18´ 9´´
26	13.2	29.3		73.3	2:46.0	18´ 11´´
27		29.2		72.9	2:45.5	19´ 0´´
28	13.1	29.1		72.5	2:45.0	19´ 2´´
29		29.0		72.1	2:44.5	19´ 4´´
30	13.0	28.9	8.0	71.7	2:44.0	19´ 5´´
31		28.8		71.3	2:43.5	19´ 7´´
32	12.9	28.7		70.9	2:43.0	19´ 8´´
33		28.6		70.5	2:42.5	19´ 10´´
34	12.8	28.5		70.1	2:42.0	20´ 0´´
35		28.4	7.9	69.7	2:41.5	20´ 1´´
36	12.7	28.3		69.3	2:41.0	20´ 3´´
37		28.2		68.9	2:40.5	20´ 4´´
38	12.6	28.1		68.5	2:40.0	20´ 6´´
39		28.0		68.1	2:39.5	20´ 8´´

105

Scale Score	100-Yd. Dash (Secs.)	220-Yd. Dash	60-Yd. Dash (Secs.)	440-Yd. Dash (Secs.)	880-Yd. Run (Min.: Secs.)	Standing Triple Jump (Ft.-In.)
40	12.5	27.9	7.8	67.7	2:39.0	20′ 9″
41		27.8		67.3	2:38.5	20′ 11″
42	12.4	27.7		66.9	2:38.0	21′ 0″
43		27.6		66.5	2:37.5	21′ 2″
44	12.3	27.5		66.1	2:37.0	21′ 4″
45		27.4	7.7	65.7	2:36.5	21′ 5″
46	12.2	27.3		65.3	2:36.0	21′ 7″
47		27.2		64.9	2:35.5	21′ 9″
48	12.1	27.1		64.5	2:35.0	21′ 11″
49		27.0		64.1	2:34.5	22′ 0″
50	12.0	26.9	7.6	63.7	2:34.0	22′ 1″
51		26.8		63.3	2:33.5	22′ 3″
52	11.9	26.7		62.9	2:33.0	22′ 4″
53		26.6		62.5	2:32.5	22′ 6″
54	11.8	26.5		62.1	2:32.0	22′ 8″
55		26.4	7.5	61.7	2:31.5	22′ 9″
56	11.7	26.3		61.3	2:31.0	22′ 11″
57		26.2		60.9	2:30.5	23′ 0″
58	11.6	26.1		60.5	2:30.0	23′ 2″
59		26.0		60.1	2:29.5	23′ 4″
60	11.5	25.9	7.4	59.7	2:29.0	23′ 5″
61		25.8		59.3	2:28.5	23′ 8″
62	11.4	25.7		58.9	2:28.0	23′ 9″
63		25.6		58.5	2:27.5	23′ 11″
64	11.3	25.5		58.1	2:27.0	24′ 0″
65		25.4	7.3	57.7	2:26.5	24′ 1″
66	11.2	25.3		57.3	2:26.0	24′ 3″
67		25.2		56.9	2:25.5	24′ 4″
68	11.1	25.1		56.5	2:25.0	24′ 6″
69		25.0		56.1	2:24.5	24′ 8″
70	11.0	24.9	7.2	55.7	2:24.0	24′ 9″
71		24.8		55.3	2:23.5	24′ 11″
72	10.9	24.7		54.9	2:23.0	25′ 0″
73		24.6		54.5	2:22.5	25′ 2″
74	10.8	24.5		54.1	2:22.0	25′ 4″
75		24.4	7.1	53.7	2:21.5	25′ 5″
76	10.7	24.3		53.3	2:21.0	25′ 7″
77		24.2		52.9	2:20.5	25′ 8″
78	10.6	24.1		52.5	2:20.0	25′ 10″
79		24.0		52.1	2:19.5	26′ 0″

Scale Score	100-Yd. Dash (Secs.)	220-Yd. Dash	60-Yd. Dash (Secs.)	440-Yd. Dash (Secs.)	880-Yd. Run (Min.: Secs.)	Standing Triple Jump (Ft.-In.)
80	10.5	23.9	7.0	51.7	2:19.0	26′ 1″
81		23.8		51.3	2:18.5	26′ 3″
82	10.4	23.7		50.9	2:18.0	26′ 4″
83		23.6		50.5	2:17.5	26′ 6″
84	10.3	23.5		50.1	2:17.0	26′ 8″
85		23.4	6.9	49.7	2:16.5	26′ 9″
86	10.2	23.3		49.3	2:16.0	26′ 11″
87		23.2		48.9	2:15.5	27′ 0″
88	10.1	23.1		48.5	2:15.0	27′ 2″
89		23.0		48.1	2:14.5	27′ 4″
90		22.9	6.8	47.7	2:14.0	27′ 5″
91	10.0	22.8		47.3	2:13.5	27′ 7″
92		22.7		46.9	2:13.0	27′ 9″
93	09.9	22.6		46.5	2:12.5	27′ 11′
94		22.5		46.1	2:12.0	28′ 0″
95	09.8	22.4	6.7	45.7	2:11.5	28′ 1″
96		22.3		45.3	2:11.0	28′ 3″
97	09.7	22.2		44.9	2:10.5	28′ 4″
98		22.1		44.5	2:10.0	28′ 6″
99	09.6	22.0		44.1	2:09.5	28′ 8″
100		21.9	6.6	43.7	2:09.0	28′ 9″

TABLE 3

Scale Score	50-Ft. Approach Triple Jump (Ft.-In.)	High Jump (Ft.-In.)	Long Jump (Ft.-In.)	Shot Put (Ft.-In.)	Mile (Min.:Secs.)	120-Yd. Low Hurdles (Secs.)
1	21′ 0″	2′ 10½″	8′ 10¼″	12′ 1″	7:13.3	:20.0
2	21′ 3″	2′ 11″	8′ 11¾″	12′ 5½″	7:11.6	:19.9
3	21′ 5½″	2′ 11½″	9′ 1¼″	12′ 10¼″	7:09.9	:19.8
4	21′ 8″	2′ 11¾″	9′ 2½″	13′ 2¾″	7:08.2	
5	21′ 11″	3′ 0½″	9′4″	13′7¼″	7:06.5	:19.7
6	22′ 1½″	3′ 1″	9′ 5½″	13′ 11¾″	7:04.8	:19.6
7	22′ 4″	3′ 1¼″`	9′ 8¼″	14′ 4½″	7:03.1	:19.5
8	22′ 6½″	3′ 1¾″	9′ 9¾″	14′ 9″	7:01.4	
9	22′ 9″	3′ 2¼″	9′ 11¼″	15′ 1½″	6:59.7	:19.4
10	23′ 0″	3′ 2¾″	10′ 0½″	15′ 6¼″	6:58.0	:19.3

Scale Score	50-Ft. Approach Triple Jump (Ft.-In.)	High Jump (Ft.-In.)	Long Jump (Ft.-In.)	Shot Put (Ft.-In.)	Mile (Min.:Secs.)	120-Yd. Low Hurdles (Secs.)
11	23′ 2½″	3′ 3¼″	10′ 2″	15′ 10¾″	6:56.3	:19.2
12	23′ 5″	3′ 3¾″	10′ 3½″	16′ 3¼″	6:54.6	
13	23′ 7½″	3′ 4¼″	10′ 4¾″	16′ 7¾″	6:52.9	:19.1
14	23′ 10″	3′ 4¾″	10′ 6¼″	17′ 0½″	6:51.2	:19.0
15	24′ 0½″	3′ 5¼″	10′ 7¾″	17′ 5″	6:49.5	:18.9
16	24′ 3½″	3′ 5¾″	10′ 9″	17′ 9½″	6:47.8	
17	24′ 6″	3′ 6¼″	10′ 10½″	18′ 2″	6:46.1	:18.8
18	24′ 8½″	3′ 6¾″	11′ 0″	18′ 6¾″	6:44.4	:18.7
19	24′ 11″	3′ 7″	11′ 1¼″	18′ 11¼″	6:42.7	:18.6
20	25′ 1½″	3′ 7½″	11′ 2¾″	19′ 3¾″	6:41.0	
21	25′ 4″	3′ 8″	11′ 4¼″	19′ 8¼″	6:39.3	:18.5
22	25′ 7″	3′ 8½″	11′ 5½″	20′ 1″	6:37.6	:18.4
23	25′ 9½″	3′ 9″	11′ 7″	29′ 5½″	6:35.9	:18.3
24	26′ 0″	3′ 9½″	11′ 8½″	20′ 10″	6:34.2	
25	26′ 2½″	3′ 10″	11′ 10″	21′ 2½″	6:32.5	:18.2
26	26′ 5½″	3′ 10½″	11′ 11½″	21′ 7¼″	6:30.8	:18.1
27	26′ 8″	3′ 11″	12′ 0¾″	12′ 11¾″	6:29.1	:18.0
28	26′ 11″	3′ 11½″	12′ 2¼″	22′ 4¼″	6:27.4	1
29	27′ 1½″	4′ 0″	12′ 3½″	22′ 8¾″	6:25.7	:17.9
30	27′ 4″	4′ 0½″	12′ 5″	23′ 1½″	6:24.0	:17.8
31	27′ 6½″	4′ 1″	12′ 6½″	23′ 6″	6:22.3	:17.7
32	27′ 9½″	4′ 1¼″	12′ 7¾″	23′ 10½″	6:20.6	
33	28′ 0″	4′ 1¾″	12′ 9¼″	24′ 3″	6:18.9	:17.6
34	28′ 2½″	4′ 2¼″	12′ 10¾″	24′ 7¾″	6:17.2	:17.5
35	28′ 5″	4′ 2¾″	13′ 0″	25′ 0¼″	6:15.5	:17.4
36	28′ 7½″	4′ 3¼″	13′ 1½″	25′ 4¾″	6:13.8	
37	28′ 10″	4′ 3¾″	13′ 3″	25′ 9½″	6:12.1	:17.3
38	29′ 1″	4′ 4¼″	13′ 4½″	26′ 2″	6:10.4	:17.2
39	29′ 3½″	4′ 4¾″	13′ 5¾″	26′ 6½″	6:08.7	:17.1
40	29′ 6″	4′ 5¼″	13′ 7½″	26′ 11″	6:07.0	
41	29′ 9″	4′ 5¾″	13′ 8¾″	27′ 3¾″	6:05.3	:17.0
42	29′ 11″	4′ 6¼″	13′ 10″	27′ 8¼″	6:03.6	:16.9
43	30′ 2″	4′ 6¾″	13′ 11½″	28′ 0¾″	6:01.9	:16.8
44	30′ 4½″	4′ 7″	14′ 1″	28′ 5½″	6:00.2	
45	30′ 7″	4′ 7½″	14′ 2¼″	28′ 10″	5:58.5	:16.7
46	30′ 9½″	4′ 8″	14′ 3¾″	29′ 2½″	5:56.8	:16.6
47	31′ 0″	4′ 8½″	14′ 5¼″	29′ 7″	5:55.1	:16.5
48	31′ 2½″	4′ 9″	14′ 6¾″	29′ 11½″	5:53.4	
49	31′ 5½″	4′ 9½″	14′ 8″	30′ 4¼″	5:51.7	:16.4

Scale Score	50-Ft. Approach Triple Jump (Ft.-In.)	High Jump (Ft.-In.)	Long Jump (Ft.-In.)	Shot Put (Ft.-In.)	Mile (Min.:Secs.)	120-Yd. Low Hurdles (Secs.)
50	31′ 8″	4′ 10″	14′ 9½″	30′ 8¾″	5:50	:16.3
51	31′ 10½″	4′ 10½″	14′ 11″	31′ 1¼″	5:48.3	:16.2
52	32′ 1″	4′ 11″	15′ 0¼″	31′ 5¾″	5:46.6	
53	32′ 3½″	4′ 11½″	15′ 1¾″	31′ 10½″	5:44.9	:16.1
54	32′ 6″	5′ 0″	15′ 3¼″	32′ 3″	5:43.2	:16.0
55	32′ 9″	5′ 0½″	15′ 4½″	32′ 7½″	5:41.5	:15.9
56	32′ 11½″	5′ 1″	15′ 6″	33′ 0″	5:39.8	
57	33′ 2″	5′ 1¼″	15′ 7½″	33′ 4¾″	5:38.1	:15.8
58	33′ 5″	5′ 1¾″	15′ 8¾″	33′ 9¼″	5:36.4	:15.7
59	33′ 7″	5′ 2¼″	15′ 10¼″	34′ 1¾″	5:34.7	:15.6
60	33′ 10″	5′ 2¾″	15′ 11¾″	34′ 6¼″	5:33.0	
61	34′ 0½″	5′ 3¼″	16′ 0½″	34′ 11″	5:31.3	:15.5
62	34′ 3″	5′ 3¾″	16′ 2½″	35′ 3½″	5:29.6	:15.4
63	34′ 5½″	5′ 4¼″	16′ 4″	35′ 8″	5:27.9	:15.3
64	34′ 8″	5′ 4¾″	16′ 5½″	36′ 0½″	5:26.2	
65	34′ 11″	5′ 4¼″	16′ 6¾″	36′ 5¼″	5:24.5	:15.2
66	35′ 1½″	5′ 5¾″	16′ 8¼″	36′ 9¾″	5:22.8	:15.1
67	35′ 4″	5′ 6¼″	16′ 9¾″	37′ 2¼″	5:21.1	:15.0
68	35′ 6½″	5′ 6¾″	16′ 11¼″	37′ 6¾″	5:19.4	
69	35′ 9″	5′ 7″	17′ 0½″	37′ 11½″	5:17.7	:14.9
70	36′ 0″	5′ 7½″	17′ 2″	38′ 4″	5:16.0	:14.8
71	36′ 2½″	5′ 8″	17′ 3¼″	38′ 8½″	5:14.3	:14.7
72	36′ 5″	5′ 8½″	17′ 3¾″	39′ 1¼″	5:12.6	
73	36′ 7½″	5′ 9″	17′ 6¼″	39′ 5¾″	5:10.9	:14.6
74	36′ 10″	5′ 9½″	17′ 7½″	39′ 10¼″	5:09.2	:14.5
75	37′ 1″	5′ 10″	17′ 9″	40′ 2¾″	5:07.5	:14.4
76	38′ 3½″	5′ 10½″	17′ 10½″	40′ 7½″	5:05.8	
77	37′ 6″	5′ 11″	18′ 0″	41′ 0″	5:03.8	:14.3
78	37′ 8½″	5′ 11½″	18′ 1¼″	41′ 4½″	5:01.4	:14.2
79	37′ 11″	5′ 11¾″	18′ 2¾″	41′ 9″	4:59.7	:14.1
80	39′ 2″	6′ 0½″	18′ 4¼″	42′ 1¾″	4:58.0	
81	38′ 4½″	6′ 1″	18′ 5½″	42′ 6¼″	4:56.3	:14.0
82	38′ 7″	6′ 4¼″	18′ 7″	42′ 10¾″	4:54.6	:13.9
83	38′ 9½″	6′ 1¾″	18′ 8½″	43′ 3¼″	4:52.9	:13.8
84	39′ 0″	6′ 2¼″	18′ 9¾″	43′ 8″	4:51.2	
85	39′ 3″	6′ 2¾″	18′ 11¼″	44′ 0½″	4:49.5	:13.7
86	39′ 5½″	5′ 3¼″	19′ 0¾″	44′ 5″	4:47.8	:13.6
87	39′ 8″	6′ 3¾″	19′ 2″	44′ 9½″	4:46.1	:13.5
88	39′ 10½″	6′ 4¼″	19′ 3½″	45′ 2¼″	4:44.4	

109

Scale Score	50-Ft. Approach Triple Jump (Ft.-In.)	High Jump (Ft.-In.)	Long Jump (Ft.-In.)	Shot Put (Ft.-In.)	Mile (Min.:Secs.)	120-Yd. Low Hurdles (Secs.)
89	40′◄″	6′4¾″	19′5″	45′6¾″	4:42.7	:13.4
90	40′3½″	6′5¼″	19′6½″	45′11¼″	4:41.0	:13.3
91	40′6″	6′5¼″	19′7¾″	46′3¾″	4:39.3	:13.2
92	40′9″	6′6¼″	19′9¼″	46′8½″	4:37.6	
93	40′11½″	6′6¾″	19′10¾″	47′1″	4:35.9	:13.1
94	41′2″	6′7″	20′0″	47′5½″	4:34.2	:12.9
95	41′4½″	6′7½″	20′1½″	47′10½″	4:32.5	:12.8
96	41′7½″	6′8″	20′3″	48′2¾″	4:30.8	
97	41′10″	6′8½″	20′4¼″	48′7¼″	4:29.1	:12.7
98	42′0½″	6′9″	20′5¾″	48′11¾″	4:27.4	:12.6
99	42′3″	6′9½″	29′7¼″	49′4½″	4:25.7	:12.5
100	42′5½″	6′10″	20′8¾″	49′9″	4:24.0	

TABLE 4. *Relationship of English to Metric Linear Measures*

One Inch	2.54	Centimeters
One Foot	30.4801	Centimeters
	.3048	Meters
One Yard	91.44	Centimeters
	.9144	Meters
One Mile (1760 Yards)	1.6093	Kilometers
One Centimeter	0.3937	Inches
One Meter	39.37	Inches
	1.0936	Yards
One Kilometer	0.62138	Miles

TABLE 5. *Comparisons of Selected Racing Distances using Metric (International) and English (American) Units*

English	Metric (English Equivalent)		
100 Yards	100 Meters (109.36 Yards)		
120 Yards (Hurdles)	110 Meters (120.296 Yards)		
220 Yards	200 Meters (218.72 Yards)		
440 Yards	400 Meters (437.44 Yards)		
800 Yards	800 Meters (874.88 Yards)		
1 Mile	1,500 Meters	(0.932	Miles or 1640.4 Yards)
	1,600 Meters	(0.994422	Miles or 1749.8 Yards)
2 Miles (Steeplechase)	3,000 Meters	(1.864 Miles)	
3 Miles	5,000 Meters	(3.1069 Miles)	
6 Miles	10,000 Meters	(6.2138 Miles)	

Suggested Reading

Bowerman, William J., and Harris, W.E. *Jogging*. New York: Grosset & Dunlap, Inc., 1967.

Cooper, Kenneth H. *The New Aerobics*. New York: Bantam Books, 1970.

Dyson, Geoffrey H.G. *Mechanics of Athletics*, 4th ed. London: University of London Press, 1967.

Mathews, Donald K., and Fox, E.L. *The Physiological Basis of Physical Education and Athletics*. Philadelphia: W.B. Saunders Co., 1971.

Olson, Edward C. *Conditioning Fundamentals*. Columbus, Ohio: Charles E. Merrill Publishing Co., 1967.

Powell, John T. *Track and Field Fundamentals*. Champaign, Illinois: Stipes Publishing Co., 1962.

Slocum, Donald B., and Bowerman, W.J. "The Biomechanics of Running." *Clin. Orthop.* 23 (1962): 39-45.

INDEX

113